THE
CRISIS
IN
THE
LIFE
OF
JESUS

Books by ERNEST F. SCOTT

THE
CRISIS
IN THE LIFE OF
JESUS

THE CLEANSING OF THE TEMPLE AND ITS SIGNIFICANCE

by

E. F. SCOTT, D.D.

1952

CHARLES SCRIBNER'S SONS

NEW YORK

PREFACE

The historical enquiry into the life of Jesus began only a century ago but has now become one of the principal fields of New Testament study. It may fairly be regarded as the most important, for our religion is founded, not on any doctrine or speculation, but on historical facts which cannot be rightly interpreted unless we know definitely what they were. Facts, however, have little meaning when each of them is taken by itself, apart from its relation to all the others. The visitor to a city is confused by the maze of streets, and ascends some tower or hill-top from which he can see at once how the city is laid out and in what surroundings. Is there anything in the Gospels which can serve as an eminence of this kind for a survey of the history of Jesus? I have long felt that we may find such an incident in the cleansing of the temple. Compared with some others this may appear a minor episode, and little attention is paid to it in the ordinary lives of Jesus. Yet it is integral with the story of the Passion, and also with

v

the narrative which has gone before. It comes at the
crucial moment when Jesus had closed his teaching
ministry and was entering on the final conflict. Like
Caesar's crossing of the Rubicon it marks a great decision, which was the outcome of the previous events and
determined those which were to follow. More than any
other act of Jesus it reveals the nature of the forces
which opposed him and at last effected his death. Not
only does it throw light on the outward history but it
supplies the key to some aspects of his thought and purpose which might otherwise remain obscure. In the
present book, I have discussed the one incident in its
larger import. All the primary questions in the history
of Jesus are involved in it—his attitude to the old religion, his claim to Messiahship, the aims of his mission,
the causes of his condemnation and death. I have tried
to show that some answer to these questions can be discovered in this significant incident. I gladly acknowledge
my debt to the authors of many commentaries and lives
of Jesus, and more particularly to E. Lohmeyer and R.
H. Lightfoot, who in recent years have dealt specially
with this subject.

E. F. Scott.

CONTENTS

THE
CRISIS
IN
THE
LIFE
OF
JESUS

Chapter One

THE GOSPELS AS HISTORY

It has often been said that no life of Jesus can ever be written, and in one sense this is true. We can have only a partial knowledge even of our nearest friends. Their inner motives and struggles are hidden from us. There have been events in their experience, often the most decisive, of which they never speak. Every human life is like the moon which only presents one side to our view, and an extraordinary life, lived long ago under conditions quite different from ours, can never be really known to us.

There might seem, however, to be particular reasons why we cannot have any but the most shadowy knowledge of Jesus. Our information is all derived from the four Gospels and much of it appears, on close analysis, to be of doubtful value. Even when they can be fully trusted these records afford us only a few occasional glimpses of Jesus. They are based on oral traditions of a fragmentary nature which had come down, for the most part, without any indication of place and time.

The evangelists have done their best to weave them together into something like a regular history, but it is largely conjectural and is full of serious gaps and contradictions. Out of this meagre, disjointed narrative it seems impossible to form any adequate conception of the life of Jesus. He must always remain a dim figure in the remote past, of whom we cannot be entirely sure whether he belongs to history or legend.

It cannot be said, however, that we have little or no material to work on in the effort to re-construct the life. The truth is rather that our information is exceptionally full. It is not too much to say that there is no character in ancient history of whom we know so much. There were indeed statesmen and warriors whose doings are described in much more detail, but besides the acts of Jesus his sayings and his private dealings with men and women are put on record and we are made to know him from within. He stands out more clearly in his living personality than any one else whose memory has been preserved. And even of his actions it is surprising how much we know. The Fourth Evangelist says at the close of his Gospel that if everything told of Jesus were put into writing, the world would not contain the books.* This is a playful exaggeration, but it bears witness to an immense number of traditions which were circulating in the church about the end of the first century. Most of them would be only the fables which grow up around a famous name, but there would also be much that was genuine, though of minor religious value.

* Jn. 21:25.

The task of the evangelists was to make a right selection out of this great mass of reminiscence. They have often been regarded as painfully gleaning the few scraps of information which were still available after the lapse of half a century, but their trouble was rather with the abundance of their material. How much of it should they leave out if they were to compile an authentic record?

So if a history of Jesus can never be written it is not because we know too little about him. The facts are before us, but how are they to be connected with each other so that we may trace the life in its continuity? This was the difficulty which was recognised from the first. Papias observes in the earliest account of the Gospels which has come down to us that Mark recorded the things concerning Jesus "accurately but not in order." It has been pointed out that this criticism of Mark is unjust, for Mark has evidently been at pains to get his facts into the proper sequence, and the other evangelists have taken his Gospel in this respect as their standard, and usually go wrong when they depart from him. But Papias is thinking not so much of a faulty arrangement as of a want of perspective. Mark recounts a number of facts just as they happened, without any attempt to show how they were related or what made them significant. For the purpose of chronology nothing is so valuable as a diary, written up from day to day, but nothing is more confusing. Before a history can be made out of the miscellaneous notices they have to be set in the larger scheme of events and viewed in the light of their causes and consequences. This is what we miss in Mark's narrative, and in the Gospels generally. We are told of many things done by Jesus but are left asking why he did them and what was their bearing on one another and on his mission as a whole.

The evangelists, it must always be remembered, did not write in a purely historical interest. The main object of all of them is expressly stated by the author of the Fourth Gospel: "That ye may know that Jesus is the Christ, the Son of God, and that believing ye may have life through his name." * For this purpose it was enough to present him vividly in a number of striking episodes so that men could feel assured that he had really lived on earth, that he had known and done the will of God, that he had exercised a saving and uplifting power. Almost to our own time the Gospel record was felt to be sufficient, and for all essential purposes it can never be superseded. But in the eighteenth century the historical sense awakened. It was realised that since Jesus had lived as a man, in a given land and period, his life had to be studied like that of any other man. He had to be placed in his environment; his actions had to be traced to their motives and so connected as to make a coherent history. The omissions and contradictions in the Gospel record now became apparent. It was perceived that beneath the apparent simplicity there were many grave problems which became ever more difficult the more they were examined. Within the last fifty years there have appeared in various countries at least a hun-

* Jn. 20:31.

dred lives of Jesus written in the historical spirit. Their
purpose is to investigate the Gospel accounts, and so to
combine and amplify their scattered episodes as to present the life as a whole. No one can deny the value of
these modern lives. Many of them are the work of profound scholars, and they all have contributed something
to our knowledge. Jesus, as he lived on earth, has become real to us as he never was before. We have learned
to appreciate the difficulties he encountered, the people
he had to deal with, the manner in which he worked.
But the interpretations are all at variance. As we pass
from one of these biographies to another we feel that
we are looking at a different person. He changes from
a prophet or apocalyptic visionary into an ethical
teacher, or a social reformer, or the leader of a national
movement. The result of our modern effort to discover
the true history of Jesus has been to plunge us into
utter confusion. We feel that we can know nothing
about him and we begin to wonder whether he ever
lived at all. The chief reason for this diversity is that
each of the writers sets out, perhaps unconsciously, with
some theory of his own in the light of which he reads
the facts. He holds a certain theology and forces everything into that framework. He believes that Jesus was
idealised by his followers, and makes it his duty to look
critically at every incident and whittle it down to the
bare minimum of fact. He is absorbed in social questions, and makes out that Jesus also was concerned with
them, to the exclusion of all else. In many of the modern
lives the figure of Jesus is almost hidden by the writer's

own shadow, and none of them leaves us wholly free
from the suspicion that a theory has been formed first,
and the facts have been adjusted to it. To a great extent
this is unavoidable, and indeed necessary. No one has
a right to approach the life of Jesus who has not already
some conception of him. A biographer of Milton must
start with the conviction that this man was a great poet.
If he decides to forget this, lest it might prejudice his
judgment, he sees none of his facts in the right propor-
tion. It has been objected to our Gospels that they were
written by men who ardently believed in the divine
mission of Jesus. Would not their account of him have
been more trustworthy if they had thrown off this pre-
conception and described his actions dispassionately, as
if they were those of any ordinary man? But a record of
that kind would have been worthless. It would have
dealt with the facts wholly from the outside. It would
not have given them more accurately, since the high calling of Jesus was part of them and the one part that
mattered. Certain assumptions are necessary before any
life of Jesus can be written, and all who have attempted
the task, in ancient or modern times, have set out from
such assumptions. But these have been formed too often,
on purely theoretical grounds. One writer starts from a
doctrine, and insists that everything must be brought
into line with it. Another holds some view as to the nature of history, or religious tradition, and so interprets
the story of Jesus. Another has studied the Gospels as
literary documents and has arrived at certain conclu-
sions as to how they came into being. From this point

of view, he examines their narrative, and decides how far it may be trusted. There is indeed a place for all these methods of approach, but they all tend to be misleading. We want to know what really happened in the life of Jesus, and cannot be satisfied when we suspect that the facts are being distorted to fit them into the given frame. Is there no way of assuring ourselves that we are on solid ground in our effort to reconstruct the life?

It may be argued that nothing is necessary but to take the record as it stands and piece the various facts together, but this is just the difficulty. All that we have is a number of separate episodes. When we try to build them up into a consistent whole they fall apart and leave us where we were. This is why so many different views have been taken of the work of Jesus. It is set before us in all those separate acts, each of them conveying its own impression, and we have to blend them as best we can. From a very early time the attempt was made to form a "harmony of the Gospels"—a single book in which every passage in the four records should find its place in a coherent whole. This, it was assumed, would enable the reader to see the many-sided life in its completeness. The effort has now been abandoned, for it was found to reduce our knowledge of Jesus to a mere jumble in which all sense of harmony was lost. If we must not set out from an abstract theory neither can we be satisfied with heaping the facts together, expecting that they will somehow connect with each other and produce a unity.

What we need is some tangible clue to guide us

through that confusion of episodes in which we feel bewildered. Progress in physical science has been mainly
due to the intensive study of particular objects, often
so minute as to seem hardly worth considering. Thinkers
in ancient times fell back on myths and speculations to
explain the process by which the earth was made. The
modern enquirer puts a drop of water or a crumb of
rock under his microscope. Here is something real, and
from the tiny fragment he spells out the mystery of the
seas and the mountains. The same method is now employed in the study of history. Something can no doubt
be learned about the remote past from legend and float-
ing tradition, but there can be no sure knowledge without a foothold, however slight, in some concrete thing,—
a tool or vessel, a mound, or a faded inscription. From
this evidence the historian feels his way towards the real
conditions of a forgotten age. In like manner scholars
are now investigating the origins of our religion. They
seek for positive facts by which they can test and revise
the old assumptions. They lay hold of a positive event,
apparently of small importance, and try to discover what
was involved in it. They fix on words and phrases, which
we now use without thinking, and consider what they
must have meant to those who devised them. Study of
this kind may be ridiculed as learned trifling, and sometimes it is little more, but it has led to far-reaching
results. By concentrating on a fact, however negligible,
you obtain a starting point from which you may travel
in many directions with the assurance that you have
something solid to lean upon.

More use should be made of this method in the enquiry into the history of Jesus. We are told many things
about him, so many that we cannot put them all together. There are many things, also, which we are not
told, and we fall back on theory or imagination to sup-
ply the vacant place. But if we are baffled by the record
when viewed as a whole, we can at least seize on some
definite action and consider it in all its bearings. One
clear fact will illuminate others which are obscure. It
will help us also to explore that background of the history to which the records afford no guidance.

Almost any incident in the life of Jesus, when fully
examined, will in some degree serve this purpose. He
was always intent on a single aim. His character was of
such a nature that it revealed itself in everything he did,
as each fragment of a crystal is a miniature of the whole.
This is one reason why the Gospel writers make so much
of scattered anecdotes, some of them of little apparent
value. They are like a series of mirrors, large and small,
all of them clearly reflecting the same face. But while
Jesus is revealed in all his actions, some of them are
more significant than others, and have more to tell us
of the nature and the conditions of his work.

There is one incident which is commonly regarded as
a minor one, and in some of the lives of Jesus is hardly
mentioned. We are told that when he came to Jerusalem
in the week that was to close with his death, his first act
was to cleanse the temple of an unholy traffic which had
forced its way into the outer court. The Gospel writers
themselves deal only briefly with the incident, which was

overshadowed in their minds by the tremendous events which were presently to follow. Later writers have treated it as a mere interruption which needs to be disregarded or explained away. Yet the more we ponder it the more we realise its vital importance. It was one of the cardinal incidents which light up the history of Jesus, alike in its earlier and its later phase. For one thing, he here expressed himself not merely in words but by an emphatic action. He acted, too, of his own initiative and not in response to a question asked or a suggestion offered by others. Moreover, he performed the act at the crisis of his life. He had come to Jerusalem to put the crown on his whole enterprise. The next day or two would decide whether he was to live or die, whether he would triumph or fail. We may be sure that in those supreme hours he would do nothing that had not some bearing on the great cause he had at heart. In the act which he then performed we may look for an answer to many perplexing questions.

Doubts have been thrown sometimes on the historical character of the incident. Jesus, we are told, was not concerned with matters of ritual. Again and again in his teaching he declares that forms of worship count for little, and one of his chief objects was to replace the old ceremonial religion with one of practical service and inner communion with God. Can we believe that he would have hazarded his life in that momentous week in order to guard the sacredness of the visible temple? Again, it is pointed out that the action described was out of keeping with his known character. He was never violent and aggressive. He sought to change men from within, and cannot be imagined on this one occasion as enforcing his will by physical compulsion. It is further argued that such an act would certainly have raised a tumult, especially at that season when thousands of excited pilgrims were gathered around the temple. But of this there is no indication. Jesus returned on the following day to the very place where he had made his angry protest and no one molested him or seemed to remember what he had done. The routine of the temple was apparently going on again as it had done before. Must we not infer on these grounds and others like them that we have here to deal, not with history, but with one of those popular legends which have intruded themselves now and then into the record? Such doubts, however, are gratuitous. The incident has found a place in all of the four Gospels—one of the very few which are so distinguished. In John's Gospel it appears with important variations, proving that this Evangelist has drawn it from a source unknown to the others. Many accounts of Jesus were in circulation, but all of them had preserved this incident, which belonged to the earliest stratum of Gospel tradition. No weight can be allowed to the argument that if the incident was authentic more would have been heard of it in the later narratives. The evangelists do not pretend to tell us everything, and there may have been a commotion of which they say nothing. But it is evident that the action of Jesus had a profound effect, for events now began to happen which had their issue in his death. The further argument that his violent cleansing of the temple is quite out of keeping with all that we know of his character is also futile. When the historian or man of science meets with one fact which seems at variance with the others, he does not rule it out. He acknowledges, rather, that his previous knowledge has been in some way defective and sees that he must revise or expand it. It is just for this reason that the unexpected action of Jesus has peculiar value. We are made to realise that there was something in him which we have not taken into account. Our conception of him must be so enlarged and modified as to make room for this element in his nature which seems in conflict with the others.

There can indeed be no better proof that the incident really happened than its seeming disagreement with the record generally. At the time when our Gospels were written the emphasis was all thrown on those aspects of Jesus which made him the perfect fulfilment of Isaiah's prophecy of the Suffering Servant. It has been noted that the later evangelists have been at pains to alter or omit those passages of Mark which describe him as angry or indignant or moved in any way by human passion, and the church cannot have invented a story which was in plain contradiction to its most cherished beliefs. If it is included in all four Gospels this can only be because it was so integral to the tradition that it could not be left out. No record of Jesus could be accepted as genuine which did not contain some reference to this well-remembered incident. It may be added that at the later time there was no reason to invent a story dealing with the temple, which had now ceased to exist. The question of its holiness was no longer of any interest, and to readers who knew nothing of the old system of worship the action of Jesus would hardly be intelligible. The story evidently goes back to a time when the venerated building was still standing, and every one was familiar with its arrangements. A minor detail in Mark's account is in this respect highly significant. He tells us that when Jesus drove out the traders and money-changers, he also forbade that any man should carry a vessel through the temple. The sacred enclosure made a great wedge into the city, and it was often convenient to go through it instead of around it on errands of ordinary business. A graphic detail of this kind would never have occurred to any legend-maker in a time when the temple had faded into a dim memory.

There can be little doubt, therefore, that the incident had a place in the Gospel tradition right on from the earliest time. By its nature it was a striking one and was vividly remembered by Jesus' followers when they looked back upon his life. Instead of questioning it we may regard it as one of the certainly authentic elements in the history. It appears in all the Gospels with variations which only show that different reports were all agreed on the main fact. It is fully in harmony with the known conditions at that particular time. It offers a picture of Jesus which was not the conventional one, and which would not have been accepted by the church, except on evidence which could not be denied. More-

over, the difficulties it presents are only on the surface.
When we study it more deeply, in its relation to the
Gospel narrative as a whole, we can see that it was fully
consistent with the purpose and the character of Jesus
and with all his recorded acts and words. There is no
fact in history on which doubt may not be thrown by
ingenious arguments, but a point comes when evidence
is irresistible. We may fairly claim that this is so in
Jesus' cleansing of the temple. The fact is certain, but
nothing is directly told us of its meaning or its connection with all that went before and after it. It raises many
problems, all of them crucial for our understanding of
the life of Jesus, but it also points the way to their solution.

Chapter Two

THE INCIDENT OF THE CLEANSING

It is one of the evils of a ceremonial religion that sooner or later it becomes commercialised. When worship is made inseparable from material objects—images, garments, relics, sacrificial victims—there must be some means of buying them, and those who can sell will make the most of their opportunity. This had happened in Judaism, which rested on the system of sacrifices laid down in the Mosaic law. Whoever appeared before God in the temple had to bring a victim to lay on his altar, if it were nothing more than a dove which could be bought for a farthing. Markets were therefore provided, and it was understood that they should be outside of the sacred precincts, but the transport of animals, even for a short distance, was difficult, especially during a great festival when all approaches were crowded. The practice had grown up of selling the victims in the outer court of the temple itself. Arrangements were likewise made for the changing of money. The imperial coins all bore the head of Caesar, and graven images, expressly forbidden in the Law, could not be used in the holy place. So the temple had a currency of its own, specimens of which can still be seen in museums, and in this coinage all dealing in sacred things had to be transacted. The outer court of the temple had thus the appearance of a busy market-place with stalls of cattle, dealers shouting their wares, and money-changers deluding the unwary.

It could not be denied that all this was a profanation but the people had now grown accustomed to it and accepted it as a matter of course. Moreover, they had always the excuse, which has covered so many dubious enterprises, that the purpose was a religious one. The purchase of the animal might fairly be regarded as part of the act of sacrifice and was thus a service rendered to God. It was required, too, that the traffic should be confined to an outer part of the temple, presumably the court of the Gentiles, who were admitted thus far into the holy building by way of privilege. So long as Israelites could worship on holy ground it could not matter that sheep and oxen were herded with Gentiles, who were much on the same level in the sight of God.

The temple was the special charge of the chief priests and they must have granted their sanction to the traffic. A large part of their revenue was no doubt derived from it. The merchant who could dispose of his goods on the very spot where they were wanted would have an advantage over his competitors, and would be glad to pay for it liberally. When we consider that sacrifices were in process all the year round, and during the great feasts would amount to thousands, we can see how the temple authorities would profit if they received only a small percentage. This aspect of the desecration would certainly be in Jesus' mind when he made his protest.

We are told, then, that when he saw the traffic in the temple court he set himself to make an end of it. He drove out the cattle-dealers and the sellers of doves. He bade the money-changers remove their tables. As he did so, he reminded the people that the temple was set apart for the worship of God and repeated words of scripture which condemned all those who profaned it. To this extent all the records are agreed. Matthew and Luke follow the account in Mark, and depart from it only at some minor points. The variations in the Fourth Gospel are more serious and seem to point clearly to a separate tradition.

The most striking difference is in the date assigned to this episode. According to the other evangelists it belonged to the final week of Jesus' ministry and began the course of events which led up to his death. John places it at the very outset. He assumes a visit to Jerusalem before Jesus was yet known as a teacher, just after the miracle at Cana by which he had first manifested his glory. The two versions cannot possibly be harmonised, and it has been held by some scholars that they deal with quite separate events. At the opening of his ministry, Jesus entered the temple and for the time being suppressed the traffic which was polluting it. He visited it again in the week of his death, and found that the old evils had revived and for a second time put them down. We cannot but feel that this explanation is forced and artificial. Two narratives which in all respects are so much alike must refer to the same event, and the only question is which of them has dated it correctly. On every ground the preference must be given to the Synoptic writers. Almost always we have to accept their guidance on matters of historical fact, and they say nothing of a visit to Jerusalem prior to the work in Galilee. Even if Jesus had made such a visit it cannot be supposed that at that time he could have interfered with the arrangements of the temple. His action was possible only when he had won for himself an authority which the people were ready to acknowledge. In the Synoptic Gospels, too, the incident comes naturally, at the point when events are mounting to a climax. In the Fourth Gospel it has no relation to anything that precedes or follows it. The evangelist knows it only as an isolated fact for which he has to find a place somewhere in the history. Why he puts it where he does is difficult to explain. Most likely, in his usual manner, he sees in it a symbolical value and for that reason couples it with the miracle of Cana. In that first of his miracles Jesus revealed his divine power and likewise in his cleansing of of the temple he made it clear that he was clothed with a higher authority. As he had changed water into wine, so he transformed the old mechanical religion into a spiritual and vital one. We may say, indeed, that the evangelist did not intend that his placing of the incident should be taken chronologically. His interest here, as

always, is in the inner meaning of the work of Jesus, and
he therefore begins his history with an incident which
serves as a kind of frontispiece, illustrating the purpose
of the work. Jesus purified the temple, showing thereby
that he had come to remove all barriers to the true
worship of God.

Apart from his dating of the incident John departs,
in several notable respects, from the Synoptic record.
For one thing, he describes Jesus as using physical violence in his expulsion of the wrong-doers. He drove
them out with a whip, and poured out the exchangers'
money and overturned their tables. We hear nothing of
all this in the other narratives, and it is obviously incredible. One man cannot have attacked a large number
in that manner, and if he had done so, he would only
have provoked resistance and defeated his own end. His
action, too, would have lost its chief significance. By
means of it he asserted his authority, as when a commanding officer by a mere word or gesture enforces his
will on a whole company. Jesus was Lord of the temple.
He gave his order and all who heard him were conscious
at once that this was their Master. The aim of the other
evangelists is to convey this impression, which is certainly the right one. Nevertheless the mention of physical violence may be due to a quite natural misunder-
standing. The crowd of onlookers would not remain
passive when Jesus issued his command. Their own
conscience would be aroused, and they would feel now,
as they had not before, that this abuse of the temple was
a sacrilege. Many willing hands would lend their assist-

ance when Jesus said "Take these things away," and
the intruders would be thrust out by no gentle means.
But the idea that Jesus himself joined in the violence
which followed his protest may on every ground be set
aside. His action found a singular parallel many cen-
turies later when Savonarola effected a cleansing of the
cathedral of Florence, which had been degraded by
frivolous uses. He did not resort to any methods of physical force, for this was unnecessary. He only spoke out
as a prophet of God, and the people confessed that he
was right and supported him. His simple word was far
more effectual than any knotted whip.

Between John's account and that of the Synoptic
Gospels there is another difference. To the incident of
the cleansing he appends the saying "Destroy this temple and in three days I will raise it up." According to
the other Gospels this saying was attributed to Jesus by
false witnesses at his trial. John is undoubtedly right
when he affirms that Jesus spoke the words or something
like them, but he cannot have done so in connection
with the cleansing. The whole purpose of that act was
to honour the temple, and he cannot have accompanied
his act with words of disparagement. There is indeed no
contradiction between his reverence for the temple and
his assertion that it was only a symbol which would
presently give place to the reality. It was his profound
sense of what the building signified which caused him
to insist that it should be kept sacred. But it is not
credible that when he thus declared the holiness of
the temple he added, almost in the same breath, "It is

nothing in itself, and I look for a time when it will be destroyed." * The saying must have been uttered on another occasion, in a different context, or it would have nullified the act.

John's account is thus at variance with those of the Synoptic writers, and these also, when they are compared, differ in some respects from one another. They are indeed in close agreement, for Matthew and Luke are both dependent on Mark, and repeat his narrative in an abridged form. But in the effort to condense it several highly important points have been obscured. Most notably, while Matthew and Luke put the cleansing on the evening of the day when Jesus entered Jerusalem, Mark is at pains to make clear that it took place on the day following. He describes how Jesus rode in from Bethany, descended the Mount of Olives and crossed the ravine, then went into the temple and "looked round about on all things." By this time it was late and he could do nothing further and made his way back to Bethany. Next morning he returned, and proceeded at once to cleanse the temple. It cannot be doubted that Mark, on whom Matthew and Luke rely, has placed the events in the right sequence, and that Jesus performed his action on the day succeeding his previous visit. This detail is all-important. It has generally been assumed that he acted on an impulse of indignation when he saw the holy place profaned, but this cannot have been. On the day before he had made

* Jn. 2:19.

a close inspection of the temple. Probably he had not
seen it since he was a boy, and in the interval it had
been largely re-built on a magnificent scale and there
would be much to look at and admire. But we may be
sure that his interest in that fateful week would not be
that of a sightseer. He examined the temple to find out
whether it was truly fulfilling its sacred purpose, and
the first thing that met his eye when he entered it was
that tumult of cattle-dealers and money-changers. At the
time he said nothing, and delayed his protest till the
next day. He must have acted, therefore, with full deliberation. He had given himself time to consider what
he should do. He had come to the city intent on a great
object but was willing to be guided by events and
circumstances in choosing his course of action. Now it
was borne in upon him that he could best commence
his work by a purification of the temple. In that first
visit when he looked round about him and saw the
conditions prevailing, he may have come to this decision, but he held himself back until he had pondered
the matter in all its bearings. Next morning he found
himself prepared to act. Thus we may gather from
Mark's account that he did not merely give way to a
rash impulse which he would possibly regret in a calmer
mood. He had allowed himself a night's rest and had
taken all the difficulties and consequences into account.
His action cannot be dismissed as one for which he was
hardly responsible since it was only the effect of a sudden shock of indignation. He knew what he was doing.
He desired in some impressive manner to inaugurate

his work in Jerusalem and was convinced, after due reflection, that he could best declare his purpose by
cleansing the temple.

In their effort to abridge the narrative of Mark the
other Synoptic writers have made a further omission
which affects the whole character of Jesus' act. Like
Mark they record the words which he quoted from
Isaiah,* "My house shall be called a house of prayer,"
but leave out the concluding words "for all nations."
They feel, apparently, that these words are superfluous
and only distract attention from the main idea. But
when we turn to the original passage in Isaiah we find
that it centers entirely about these closing words. The
prophet is looking to a time when "the sons of the
stranger who give themselves to the Lord" will share in
the blessing of Israel. "Even them will I bring to my
holy mountain, and make them joyful in my house of
prayer, for my house shall be called a house of prayer
for all peoples." * Jesus would undoubtedly have the
whole prophecy in his mind, and when he quoted it,
would lay the emphasis on those words which Matthew
and Luke omit. He recalled it, we may well believe, for
the sake of those words which pointed its meaning. The
sale of cattle was held in the court of the Gentiles on
the assumption that this was no real part of the temple.
God was concerned only with his favoured people.
When Gentiles prayed, he would not hear them, and
the place assigned to them could be treated as unhal-
lowed ground. Jesus declared that those who thought

* Isai. 56:7.

in this manner had never realised the purpose of the temple, or the purpose of God for whose service it existed. It was a house of prayer for all nations, and all had a right to pray to the common Father. Incidentally, we have here a striking proof that the story of the cleansing is authentic. The church cannot have invented it, for the church was blind, apparently, to an essential part of its meaning.

It may further be observed that Mark has perceived the importance of the incident, as Matthew and Luke have failed to do. They bring it in quite casually, as an appendix to their account of the triumphal entry. Mark gives it a place by itself as the first and most striking of the events that led up to Jesus' death. He is aware, too, that it was vitally connected with the tragedy, for he tells us that immediately afterwards the chief priest met in council and decided that Jesus must die. They were already hostile to him, but it was this act in the temple which finally determined them. John has put the incident in the wrong setting and does not appreciate its bearing on the historical facts, but in his own way he sees its significance, even more clearly than Mark. He singles it out as the act by which Jesus asserted his divine authority. He suggests that from that time onward the old type of religion, based on ordinances and material things, gave way to the true spiritual worship. For John, the cleansing of the temple was no mere outward event which had to be given its place in the history of Jesus. It revealed the inner purpose of his mission,

and had therefore to stand at the beginning so that all
that followed could be viewed in the light of it.

The four accounts thus differ at important points, but
when they are sifted and compared, the main facts
appear to stand out clearly. Jesus had arrived in Jerusalem and had presented himself like other pilgrims in
the temple. He was shocked to find that the outer court
had been turned into a market, but on this preliminary
visit he said nothing. Next day, however, he returned
from Bethany, where he had arranged to stay during the
feast, and carried out the design which had now formed
in his mind. With a voice of authority he commanded
the traffickers to be gone, taking their cattle with them.
He declared that the temple was a house of prayer, not
only for Israelites but for all who were seeking after
God. The holy place, he said, had become a den of
thieves. By this he did not insinuate that the traders
were doing their business dishonestly, though it is more
than likely that most of them took all the advantage
they could of the ignorant strangers. They were thieves
because they were robbing God of the honour due to
him by using his house for unholy purposes. All who
listened to Jesus' protest, and even the traffickers themselves, were conscious that he was right. Merchants and
exchangers began to slink away, and their departure
was hastened by rough usage on the part of the crowd.
At least for that hour the temple was cleared of sacrilege.
How long the change remained effectual we do not

know. There is no indication in the subsequent part of
the narrative that conditions in the temple became different, but it is probable that for a short time the intruders were afraid to outrage the public feeling which
Jesus had aroused. But before the week was over he had
been put to death as a false prophet, and his work was
all discredited. Those who had supported him would
now be ashamed that they had yielded so easily, and the
traffic would be resumed, much as before. The temple
worship all hinged on animal sacrifice, and most people
would be glad to secure their offerings in the most convenient way. So long as the material type of worship
existed it was bound to encourage abuses. The system
itself was at fault and the temple needed to be not only
purified but destroyed, so that a different kind of worship might take its place. Jesus made this plain in his
memorable saying, and he would not have risked his life
only to make some temporary improvement in the ceremonial religion which had had its day. He was intent
on his own mission and on the manner in which it
might be accomplished. He thought of the temple as in
some way significant for that mission, and to understand
his action we must consider it in its larger context. What
had he been doing in that whole period which had preceded his coming to Jerusalem? How was his earlier
work related to his action in the temple?

Chapter Three

THE CLEANSING AND THE MINISTRY

The incident in the temple appears to stand by itself, breaking in upon a narrative which would lose nothing if it were dropped out. This is one of the reasons why its authenticity has been doubted, and its origin sought in legend or in some forgotten controversy which agitated the early church. Even when accepted as historical, it has been treated as a mere accident in the career of Jesus, due to an impulse which deflected him for a moment from his normal course of action. We may be sure, however, that in those critical days when his whole cause was at hazard he did nothing unthinkingly, and Mark expressly tells us that he acted after a night's reflection. If the incident seems inconsistent with the history as a whole, this can only mean that our view of the history has been inadequate, and must be re-adjusted to allow for this action which is integral with all the others.

It cannot be affirmed too strongly that the Passion was part of the ministry of Jesus. Too often we detach it, more or less consciously, and think of the life as sharply

divided. Jesus had worked in Galilee as a wandering
teacher, then he suddenly came forward in a new character and began an enterprise quite different from that
which had occupied him hitherto. This is improb-
able, and when we study the record more closely it is
manifestly wrong. During his journey to Jerusalem
Jesus had continued his previous work of teaching. He
was welcomed on his arrival as the prophet from Naz-
areth in Galilee. It was in this character that he was
called on to give his judgment on a number of doubtful
questions, and he answered them in the manner already
familiar to his followers. To his own mind the work on
which he was now entering was continuous with that
which he had previously done, and we must not make a
division which he never made himself. The two parts of
his life must be taken together, and each of them has to
be explained, at every point, in its relation to the other.
It is necessary, therefore, to consider, at least in its
broad outline, the course of that ministry which cul-
minated in the Passion week.

Jesus had set himself, then, to proclaim the Kingdom
of God and pursued this work for a period of perhaps a
year and a half in his native province of Galilee. Almost
from the outset he had made a deep impression and had
won a large following. His fame had spread not only
through Galilee but over the whole country, and at the
same time he had aroused a strong and ever-growing
opposition. The religious leaders were bitterly hostile to
his teaching, which was contrary, they clearly perceived,

to the fundamental principles of the Law. In Palestine, too, a religious movement always tended to merge in a political one, and this danger was more acute than ever at that time when pious Israelites were chafing under their subjection to a heathen power. It was the chief difficulty of Jesus that he had to carry on a purely religious work in a heated political atmosphere. His whole interest was in the coming Kingdom of God, but the people, for the most part, could not separate his message from the national issue.

He had thus to encounter a double opposition, from the side of orthodox Judaism and from that of the constituted government. We hear much in the Gospels of his controversies with the scribes and Pharisees, and the impression is left on us that they were mainly responsible for the final tragedy. But behind them there were other adversaries who were suspicious of him on political grounds. The spirit of revolt was in the air and a man who had become a popular hero, whatever he professed to be his aims, was politically dangerous. It was for this reason, according to Josephus, whose evidence may here be relied on, that Herod Antipas had John the Baptist thrown into prison and murdered. The Gospel writers tell us that Herod sought the life of Jesus, not because of his teaching, for which he probably cared nothing, but because he was exciting the multitude. Jesus left Galilee abruptly to escape the plots of this petty tyrant who could do nothing outside of his small domain; but he had to reckon with a more serious danger. The ultimate authority in Palestine was the Roman government, which was always on its guard in that turbulent province against any possible menace to its sovereignty.

Rome, however, had soon discovered that the Jews were a race by themselves, with traditions and institutions which no foreigner could understand, and it was content to administer Palestine through native authorities. It had fixed on the higher orders of the priesthood as the nearest approach in this strange country to a governing class. The national life was all centred on the temple at Jerusalem, and the priests had charge of the temple. It seemed natural to entrust them with civil as well as religious duties on condition that they should act in the name of Rome and protect the Roman interests. To ensure their fidelity, the life-tenure of the high-priesthood was abolished, and the office changed hands every few years at the discretion of the imperial power. The priests were never allowed to forget that they ruled as the delegates of Rome. They knew that if there was any disquiet they would be held responsible and were anxious to keep all conditions as they were.

The mission of Jesus was a religious one, and he was at pains to avoid all matters that might involve him in political quarrels. He seems to have been well-disposed to the Roman government which had brought order and prosperity to his country, and there is no sign that it put any difficulties in his way. Until he was finally set before Pilate for trial his name was probably unknown to any official from Rome. But we may be sure that he was under close supervision by the chief priests and

their retainers. He was the leader of a popular movement, and it was out of such movements that trouble
had always arisen. As yet he had confined himself to
Galilee which had its own local king and was outside of
the jurisdiction of the ruling council at Jerusalem. Yet
the council would keep its eye on events in Galilee,
which had long been notorious as a centre of disaffec-
tion. A rising in Galilee could not fail to spread beyond
it and should be suppressed, if possible, at its source.
We hear little in the earlier part of Jesus' ministry of
priestly intervention, though Mark has preserved a significant notice of "Scribes who had come down from
Jerusalem," * and tells how the Pharisees "Took coun-
sel with the Herodians against him." † The authorities
in the capital plainly had their emissaries at work, and
if they seemed not to interfere it was only because they
kept their activities in the background. We know from
the detailed history in Josephus that the chief priests
were masters of intrigue and always employed the under-
hand method in preference to the open one. That they
so acted in their attack on Jesus comes out very clearly
in the record of the Passion week, and we may safely
assume that they had been working on similar lines long
before. If all were known, it would be found that the
opposition to him in Galilee had been inspired or at
least fomented by the priestly council in Jerusalem.

The surest way to weaken his influence on the people
was to make them doubtful of his religion. If it could be

* Mk. 3:22.
† Mk. 3:6.

shown that he despised the Law, that his demands were
contrary to scripture, that he was possessed with an evil
spirit, the popular reverence would quickly change to
abhorrence. It was the Pharisees who assailed him on
the religious side, and it cannot be questioned that their
opposition to him was sincere. They could indeed find
little in his words or conduct that was definitely wrong.
They could only accuse him of trifling breaches of the
Sabbath law, of friendships with men and women who
were ritually unclean, of doubtful interpretations of
texts of scripture. Yet Rabbis of the highest standing
had taken much the same position as he did on all these
matters, and no one had thought of condemning them.
It was not any tangible error in his teaching that was
repugnant to the Pharisees but his whole temper and
outlook. They perceived, more clearly perhaps than he
did himself, that if his spirit prevailed there would be
no place for the Law, which they accepted as the final
word of God.

Apart, however, from this vague sense that the teaching of Jesus was dangerous the Pharisees had no serious
charge against him. There were open-minded men
among them who admired him and were in sympathy
with his ideas. It is difficult to account for the bitter
enmity with which many of them regarded him. We
cannot but surmise that some pressure had been applied
to them aggravating the suspicions which they felt on
religious grounds. It had been represented to them that
he was a public enemy, that he was hiding dark designs
under cover of a harmless message, that his removal was

necessary for the common good. There was only one quarter from which suggestions of this kind could have come. Pharisees and Sadducees, the defenders of the Law and the partisans of the priesthood, were in opposite camps; but in the attack on Jesus we find them working together, and this collusion had evidently begun long before he arrived in Jerusalem. The priests had sent their agents into Galilee, as soon as the new teacher had become notorious, to ensure that the local Pharisees should do their part in suppressing him. In the priestly opposition there was a political motive which counted for little with the Pharisees. "This man," said Caiaphas, "doeth great miracles, and if we let him alone the Romans will come and take away both our place and nation." The passage in the Fourth Gospel * which records this speech of the high-priest is based undoubtedly on authentic knowledge. Yet it would be unjust to think of Caiaphas and his colleagues as nothing but political schemers, wrapped up in their worldly interests. They could not forget that they were the official heads of the national religion and they felt, like the Pharisees, that it was now in danger. The statesmen who fought against the Reformation had, no doubt, political ends in view but they must not be condemned as mere crafty politicians. They were religious men who believed sincerely that they were standing for the true faith, and we must allow for a similar mixture of motives in the priestly rulers who opposed Jesus. They saw in him a menace to the existing government and to

* Jn. 11:49.50.

their own privileges but they also had the cause of religion at heart. It was in no hypocritical spirit that they
joined hands with the defenders of the Law.

It may be assumed, then, that they took part from the
first in the opposition to Jesus and in great measure
inspired it. They remained in the background and did
not actively interfere until the closing days. It might
appear that till then they were hardly aware of what
Jesus had been doing. This, however, is quite incredible
since they were accountable to Rome for the peace of
the country, which was plainly threatened by the excitement now spreading in Galilee. From the outset
they must have taken note of the new Prophet, and as
his influence grew ever more apparent, they must have
grown seriously alarmed. By every means in their power
they would try to frustrate his work. This must be
borne in mind when we consider his action in the temple. It seems to be quite unrelated to anything that has
gone before and the question has often been raised as
to why, at the very crisis of his life, he went out of his
way, without any provocation, to create for himself a
new and terrible group of enemies. His quarrel had
been only with the scribes and Pharisees and had turned
wholly on matters of the Law. The priests, who were
only concerned with the administration of the temple,
had never crossed his path, but now he apparently forgot his proper adversaries and performed an act which
was certain to enrage the all-powerful priesthood. But
nothing ever happens without a cause, and if Jesus

cleansed the temple, the reason must be sought in the previous history.

As we look back, then, on Jesus' work in Galilee two things stand out unmistakably. On the one hand, he achieved a marvellous success. Coming forward as an unknown man he had made himself recognised in a few months' time as a great prophet, a leader in Israel. It has been inferred from vague statements in the Fourth Gospel that the enthusiasm he had at first awakened had quickly died down, and that latterly he had been abandoned by most of his following and ended his life in loneliness and apparent failure. This is certainly a mistaken view. All the indications show that his fame and influence were continually growing. Of this we have convincing proof in the very fact that he was crucified. If he had manifestly failed, there would have been no object in thus destroying him. It would have been the height of folly for the revered chiefs of the nation to hand over to Roman execution a harmless fellow-countryman whose cause was already lost. They would have brought themselves into odium and contempt, and all for nothing. But they had him put to death because no other course was open to them. He had won a position which made him extremely dangerous. His success had been so great that if it increased much further they would be helpless against him, and they felt, therefore, that they must accept all risks and act at once. Their procedure cannot be explained in any other way.

But while his ministry had been highly successful, it had also called forth a fierce opposition, and to this extent it is true that in the later days he was left solitary. He was conscious after a certain point that the hostile forces were too strong for him and that his mission was failing. One of the problems in the history is his abrupt departure from Galilee just when his work appeared most flourishing. He suddenly arose, we are told, and made his way by the nearest route to the frontier,* and wandered for a while in the heathen region that lay north of Palestine. One reason for this strange flight was almost certainly his pressing need for safety. He had learned that Herod had laid plans for his murder,† and attempts of this kind may have been made already. But it is evident from the sequel that he was under an inward as well as an outward compulsion. He travelled in company with his disciples along the coast of Tyre and Sidon, and then round the base of the Lebanon mountains, apparently without aim and keeping his movements hidden. Then we find him again near the city of Caesarea Philippi, at the source of the river Jordan. It was there that he confided to the disciples that he was no other than the promised Messiah. Hitherto he had spoken only of the Kingdom of God and had said nothing of himself and his own relation to it. Even when John the Baptist had sent messengers from his prison urging him to say definitely whether he was the Coming One, he had refused to answer. Why he

* Mk. 7:24.
† Lk. 13:31.

preserved this silence we can only guess, for it is impossible to penetrate the secret mind of Jesus, but some partial parallel can be found in the life of every great hero or liberator. He begins with an inborn love of freedom and a passionate desire to work for it; then he becomes conscious of a personal call. It is borne in upon him that if this thing is ever to be accomplished he must do it himself. The abstract cause becomes incarnate in his own life and deed. So as Jesus proclaimed the Kingdom of God it grew ever clearer to him that he must himself bring in the Kingdom. This was the task to which God had appointed him and there was only one way in which he could express this conviction in the terms of Jewish thought. The prophets had foretold a Messiah who would appear in the latter days and establish a reign of God. Jesus was now assured that these prophecies pointed to himself.

It has been argued at various times that he was the victim of some kind of megalomania. As he grew ever more conscious of his powers, and multitudes thronged to him and acclaimed him, he was carried away by wild ambitions and nothing would satisfy him at last but to offer himself as the Messiah. But it is evident from the record that he assumed the title unwillingly. He thought of Messiahship not as a prize but as a terrible responsibility. He saw clearly that it would involve him in suffering and death, and he would fain have avoided it. In many ways, too, the Messianic conception was alien to his own sense of what God required of him. The Messiah foretold in scripture was to be a king like David,

who would deliver Israel from its enemies and make it
the foremost of all nations. This was the Coming One
whom the people expected, and Jesus could not identify
himself with hopes which were contrary to all his knowledge of God's purposes. Yet it was the Messiah who was
to bring in the Kingdom of God and since he felt this
to be his appointed task he could not doubt that he was
the Messiah. As long as he could he resisted the conviction but it forced itself on him with a growing certainty.
We are to think of that period of wandering beneath
the northern mountains as similar to the earlier one
when he was tempted in the wilderness. He was struggling then to decide how he should carry on the mission
to which God had called him, and he was now ponder-
ing a decision which was still more momentous. Was he
to accept the Messianic office with all its fearful obliga-
tions? At last he threw aside all his hesitation and at
Caesarea Philippi made the great confession to his
chosen disciples, enjoining on them at the same time
that they were to keep it secret. He wished to be still
free to make his own declaration, at his own time and
in his own way.

From this moment it seems to have been his fixed re-
solve to go up to Jerusalem. The sequence of events is
somewhat confused in all our Gospels but it is evident
that although he returned to Galilee he did not resume
his public ministry. Mark expressly tells us that he took
care not to let his presence be generally known.* He
only remained long enough to meet some of his trusted

* Mk. 9:30.

friends, probably to arrange with them that they should go to Jerusalem to support him. It cannot have been by mere accident that when he reached the city a number of his Galilean followers, both men and women, were already there. From Galilee he set out for Jerusalem, taking the longer but easier route that lay east of the Jordan. It was a three or four days' journey but he allowed himself a considerably longer time, proclaiming his message by the way. He had evidently planned to arrive in the city just at the beginning of the Passover feast, which was not yet due.

Why did he make this fateful journey to Jerusalem? According to one view he foresaw the end and went up deliberately to die. Certainly he was fully aware of the possible consequences. His disciples remembered ever afterwards that he had set his face stedfastly and did not walk beside them, freely conversing as he was wont to do, but went on alone, and as they followed they were afraid.* Yet the event was still uncertain, and we know that up to the very last he thought it possible that the cup might be spared him. So it has sometimes been held that he looked forward to a triumph, and that the disaster fell upon him as a dreadful surprise. But the truth is, we can hardly doubt, that as yet he could see nothing certainly. In all human probability his enemies would prove too strong for him and he would suffer death, but it might be that God would uphold him in some miraculous way and give him victory. He was prepared for either event. He only knew that God required him to

* Mk. 10:32.

face his enemies in Jerusalem. He placed himself utterly
in the hands of God, and was resolved, whatever might
be the issue, to accept his will.

One thing may be taken as unquestionable, that his
going to Jerusalem had some connection with the secret
he had divulged to his disciples. It has been held that
he only made this journey as he had made others before.
Now that he had ceased to be a mere provincial figure
it was natural that he should seek a wider field and pur-
sue his work in the capital. But from the moment that
he confessed himself to be the Messiah his plans must
all have been determined by this conviction. If he
changed his sphere of work it must have been because
the work itself had taken a new direction. He had not
only to announce the Kingdom of God but to assert
himself as the Messiah through whom it would come in,
and this he could only do in Jerusalem. This was the
holy city where God had set his temple, the city in
which the prophets had died and on which the hopes of
the people had ever been centred. It was at Jerusalem
that the Messiah must reveal himself, and the fitting
time was the week of Passover when the nation was
assembled in the presence of God.

It may be that he had designed to make some formal
announcement, but there is no indication that he ever
did so. To many, this has appeared strange, and even
suspicious. They have inferred that Jesus himself never
claimed to be the Messiah and that his disciples had
misunderstood him. Others have supposed that he was
waiting to make his proclamation on the great day of

the feast, and that his enemies guessed his purpose and forestalled him. But it is not necessary to assume that he meant to declare in a public speech on a set occasion that he was the Messiah. During his ministry he had never advertised himself but had allowed his deeds to speak for him. When John's disciples had come to him with their question he had only said "Go and tell John what things you have heard and seen." We may well believe that in those closing days he was content to follow the same course. A declaration in words would have carried no weight with those who doubted him. If he was truly the Messiah he must show it by actions which would be their own evidence. It would be in keeping with all that we know of Jesus if he had planned to declare himself in this manner at Jerusalem, and if he began with the significant action of cleansing the temple.

His act must thus be viewed in its connection with the whole ministry which had gone before. The Passion week, of which it marked the opening, was only the culmination of that far longer period during which Jesus had proclaimed his message and become ever more fully conscious of the task appointed him. Paul, indeed, fixes his mind on the death of Christ, and seems to regard it as an event that stands wholly by itself; but when we look deeper into his thought we can see that he relates the death to all that he knew of Jesus—his love and compassion, his faith in God, the manner in which he had lived himself and taught his followers to live. It was the whole work of Jesus which had given significance to his

death. For all Christians since, the Cross has been bound
up inseparably with the life that preceded it. They have
realised that it summed up and brought to a focus all
that Jesus had been and all that he had done and taught.
In this light we must regard the cleansing of the temple.
It connects itself with the story of the Passion but also
with that of the earlier ministry. We must place it in
that connection before we can rightly understand its
significance.

For one thing it was made possible by the work which
Jesus had done in Galilee. It has sometimes been
thought incredible that he should have dared to act as
he did, entering the temple and commanding that a
long-established custom should be changed. How could
he have expected that any one would listen to him?
Could he have enforced his will, as we are asked to believe, without any remonstrance on the part of the
crowd? But we must remember that he had not come to
Jerusalem as an unknown man. Every one had heard
of him and had learned to think of him as a prophet,
endowed with strange powers. He was able to reckon on
this reverential attitude on the part of the onlookers.
He had behind him the influence he had gained and the
rumours which were everywhere current, and could assume the tone of authority as his natural right. It was
in virtue of his past ministry that he could venture on
this bold act in the temple. In another it would have
seemed a mere presumption but nothing could be denied to this extraordinary man.

Again, by denouncing the unholy traffic he indicted

the chief priests who had sanctioned it. He would not have done so unless he already had some ground for opposing them. Intent as he was on his own work, he was always careful to avoid conflicts which did not directly concern him. The nation was divided into sects and parties, and he was constantly pressed to take sides on one disputed issue and another, but he held aloof. He would not of his own initiative have sought a quarrel with the priesthood. Whatever might have been his indignation at the sacrilege in the temple he would have restrained it or expressed it in some other way rather than make enemies of a venerable group of men who had never offended him. We cannot but infer that he had good reason for setting himself against them. Although he was now encountering them for the first time he knew that they were his enemies, who were bent on ruining his cause. His action has thus to be explained from events in his ministry. Apart from a few vague suggestions our record says nothing of an opposition directed from Jerusalem, but Jesus must have been fully aware of it and must have realised that it was more deadly than any other. One of his motives in coming to the city, and perhaps the principal one, must have been to confront his chief enemies in their stronghold.

His action had these outward connections with the ministry before, but it also connects with the inner history of Jesus, with the purposes and convictions which determined all his earlier work. Most notably it was the act by which he finally asserted his Messiahship. The sense of his supreme calling had been gradually deepening and growing more clear and certain while he worked in Galilee. It was only at Caesarea Philippi that he made his confession, but the knowledge that he was Messiah had in some degree been always present to him. The key to his whole life may be found in this—that from the very first he was feeling his way towards the full consciousness of what he was. Not only did he become convinced that he was the Messiah, but he discerned, as the prophets had never done, what true Messiahship must be. He revised the whole Messianic idea in the light of his own knowledge of God. It was by his cleansing of the temple that he expressed the certainty to which he had now attained, that he was the Messiah who must order the house of God.

His act was the assertion of his Messianic claim, and we shall have to consider it in this aspect, but it also was related to the message he had always been proclaiming. At first sight it seems difficult to believe that he who presided at that scene of violence in the temple was also he who had spoken the parables and the Sermon on the Mount. The contrast has grated on many devout readers of the Gospels. Yet when we look at it more attentively, this act of Jesus was in full harmony with his teaching. It impresses on us in concrete form a truth which is fundamental to his ethic, and gives it a character which is altogether unique. He thought of man's life in its whole extent as the service of God and demanded, therefore, that it must base itself on reverence, on the sense that we are living ever in God's presence. When the sense of God dies out or is in any way corrupted our life is deprived of its purpose and meaning. In spite of our best efforts we can only go astray. This is the conviction that underlies all that Jesus taught us about love and justice and mercy and forgiveness. His primary concern was not with ethical principles but with worship, with that attitude to God which will govern all our efforts to serve him. So when he came to proclaim his message at Jerusalem his first act was to cleanse the temple. In a real sense all his message was included in that act without which all that he had to say would be unintelligible. The temple, to be sure, was only a house of wood and stone and his solicitude for it might seem contrary to all that we know of his purely spiritual aims. Before we can appreciate his action in its deeper implications we must pause for a little and consider what the temple meant for Jesus.

Chapter Four

JESUS' ATTITUDE TOWARDS THE TEMPLE

It might seem from our record of his teaching that Jesus concerned himself little with the temple. He never even mentions it, except in two or three quite casual references. "Which is greater, the gold or the temple which sanctifies the gold?" * "Two men went into the temple to pray, a Pharisee and a publican." † "The priests on the sabbath profane the temple and are blameless." ‡ He speaks constantly of the Law, but the temple, apparently, is hardly ever in his mind. Not only so, but again and again he utters warnings against the piety which consists only in outward ceremonies. Men must seek an inward fellowship with God; they must prove their devotion to him by their actual lives. A religion of this kind had nothing in common with that of the temple, which based itself on stated offerings and

---

* Matt. 23:17.
† Lk. 18:10.
‡ Matt. 12:5.

traditional rites. Those who listened to the Sermon on the Mount could never have been led to the reflection, "The zeal for God's house has consumed him."

The cleansing has therefore been interpreted in two ways. According to one view it must be regarded as a sort of parable in action. Jesus had no interest in the temple itself but wished to enforce a moral or spiritual truth and did so, in his usual way, by an illustration. He was in the temple, which was dedicated to the service of God, and a commerce for worldly gain had intruded into it. For himself the temple meant nothing, but to the people it was the holy place, and he sought to impress on them that the higher interests must not be confused with the earthly. Others would insist that it was the temple itself that Jesus cared for. He indeed held liberal opinions but remained at heart a devout Jew. The temple and its worship were sacred to him, and when he saw the holy building profaned all his deepest feelings were aroused and he protested at the risk of his life. The incident thus viewed has been used as a corrective to that idea of Jesus which Christian teachers, from Paul and the evangelists onward, have imposed on us. Essentially, we are told, he was a Jewish Rabbi, and in the attempt to broaden his religion into a universal one this aspect of it was carefully disguised. One episode, however, was so notorious that it had to be included in the history, and it betrays the purely Jewish Character of Jesus' mind. He saw the temple profaned and was touched to the quick. He forgot for the moment all that he had taught as to the futility of mere ritual worship and gave expression to his inner convictions.

Now it cannot be denied that in this reading of the incident there is a measure of truth. Jesus never shook off the religion into which he had been born, and this is fully recognised in the Gospel record. The evangelists do not try to conceal the Jewish elements in his teaching. On the contrary, they are at pains to present him vividly in his relation to the people among whom he lived and with whose beliefs he was in sympathy. His zeal for the temple was no pretence. He had been trained from childhood to think of it as God's house, and his early pieties clung to him and were precious, as they are to every man of noble temper. The only anecdote of his youth which has come down to us is that of his visit to the temple when he was twelve years old, and it was then, we are given to understand, that the sense of his high calling first dawned in him. We cannot wonder that the temple was associated ever afterwards with his holiest memories and aspirations.

We cannot doubt, however, that his attachment to it was much more than a sentimental one. When he spoke of it as the house of prayer for all nations he was not using the language of a pious tradition which had ceased to have any meaning to himself. He took for granted that in this building as nowhere else men had access to God, and a feeling of this kind was not inconsistent with his belief that God was present everywhere to those who truly sought him. So long as God is conceived only as an abstract idea he cannot be truly worshipped. There needs to be something that makes him real to you, some experience in which you have felt him near, some place or object which brings home to you the fact of his presence. It has often been remarked that Judaism developed out of a temple religion into a religion of the Law, and this has been regarded as a spiritual advance. In the earlier days everything had centred on a material house in which God was supposed to dwell, but as time went on the building became ever less important. It was preserved, and its service was carried on with splendid accompaniments. The people believed that in some way their destinies were bound up with it, but it was only a survival from primitive times, and its final destruction was a positive blessing. Judaism had grown into the religion of the Law. It was no longer held down to one particular place but consisted in the faithful observance of certain rules of living which could be practised anywhere. By the removal of the temple it was left free to fulfil itself as a moral and personal religion.

There is certainly much that is true in this reading of Jewish history. A religion that is localised and tied down to set conditions of worship can never adjust itself to new circumstances and larger needs. Judaism was emancipated when it learned to put the Law in the place once occupied by the temple. Yet the fact remains that it was never so much a vital religion as in the days when it centred on the temple. The best evidence of this is the book of Psalms, which were made for the temple worship. No other book has been so universal in its appeal. It expresses the religious spirit at its purest,

and the Christian church has always accepted it as the
vehicle of its devotion. Yet it comes to us from that
period when Judaism was a temple religion. It is full
of passionate allusions to the building and the priesthood and the sacrifices, even to the furniture that
adorned the holy place. One might think it impossible
that this joy in material things should have any spiritual
value, but it is in the book of Psalms that Old Testament religion becomes most truly spiritual. The reason
can only be that the temple worship evoked the feeling
for what is vital in religion. It is well to magnify the
law of God, but the chief thing necessary is to realise
his presence. In the building consecrated to him where
he was believed in some manner to have his dwelling-
place, men were able almost to touch and see him. They
could think of him as the living God.

For Jesus the temple had the same meaning that it
had for the psalmists. It was through them, indeed, that
he had formed his conception of it. He had lived at a
distance from the actual building and perhaps had never
seen it since that visit in his boyhood. But he was familiar with the Psalms and the other scriptures, written in the days when all thoughts of God were associated
with his temple. It had become idealised in his mind,
and he was bitterly disillusioned when he saw it turned
into a place of merchandise. He wished to make it a
little more like that house of God of which psalmists
and prophets had spoken. It is utterly false to suppose
that when he cleansed it he merely identified himself
for a moment with popular sentiments which he had

himself outgrown. He revered the temple. He was in the fullest sympathy with those who found help in their spiritual life from its worship. They felt as they waited in this house that God was real and that they had drawn near to him, and was not this the essential meaning of religion?

We can thus understand why Jesus, in the course of his teaching, leaves the temple alone. It is always the Law that he deals with when he criticises the religion of his time and this may seem strange, for the temple, at least formally, was still the prime object of Jewish devotion. Prayer had to be offered with the face turned towards Jerusalem. God's covenant with his people was renewed year by year through the sacrifice offered by the high-priest in the temple. The highest religious privilege was to enter its courts as a pilgrim. Yet Jesus never protests against this veneration of the temple, which lay open, one might think, more than anything else, to his condemnation. He speaks only of the Law, and of the danger of substituting its precepts for the true will of God. But he is silent on the temple because he accepts it, in spite of all that was external in its worship, as representing something that was of infinite value. The Law was concerned with the conduct of the religious life. The temple stood for religion itself. It was the visible reminder that God was present and was the one reality. To impress this on men was the inspiring motive of Jesus' own message.

He thus acknowledged the temple, and in purifying it he gave expression to a genuine reverence. To many

it has seemed inexplicable that he made so much of the
sanctity of a mere building. He had denounced the
Pharisees who paid such heed to all the minutiae of
religious practice, cleansing the outside of the cup while
it was foul within. Was he not doing much the same
when he treated a small defect in the arrangements of
the temple as if it were a matter of the deepest consequence? He showed himself less broad-minded than the
priests themselves, who were willing to relax the strict
practice of earlier times in order to make it easier for
devout worshippers to offer their sacrifices. It seems
hardly possible to think of Jesus as the zealous champion of the temple and all the details of its ritual. But
two things must be borne in mind. On the one hand, he
was not opposed to ritual for its own sake. The idea
grew up in early days and has asserted itself ever and
again in Christian history, that worship is impure if it
allows any appeal to the senses. The external element
in it must be reduced to the barest minimum before it
can be acceptable to God. But this, it must be insisted,
was not the attitude of Jesus. He indeed rejected all
forms in so far as they were merely forms, and were substituted for the thing they signified. But he maintained
that the object of worship is to make contact with God,
and that anything that has this effect is true worship.
The quiet fellowship of two or three, the enthusiasm
of a great assembly, the emotions stirred by music and
architecture, a magnificent ritual or none at all—they all
have their place. Any form of worship is right so long
as it creates in you the sense that you are in the presence

of God. Two men went into the temple to pray. One of them, even in that holy place, was absorbed in himself and was not seeking to commune with God or to ask anything of him. The other was made conscious in that glorious house that he was face to face with God and offered a prayer which God heard and answered. In this parable we can discern the attitude of Jesus to ritual worship. He held that it was worthless if you trusted only to the forms. If you have in you the spirit of worship, the forms will themselves be full of meaning and will help you to make your approach to God.

So there is another thing which must be borne in mind when we try to explain Jesus' attitude to the temple. He reverenced it because he looked beyond it to what it represented. A patriot salutes the flag of his country and rises in anger if it is insulted. You may say that this is a childish sentiment and that love of country has nothing to do with a rag of cloth. The soldier who dies for his flag on the battle-field thinks otherwise. He sees in it all that it signifies—his country and its glorious past and its future, now depending on his fidelity. It was in that manner that Jesus regarded the temple. Though it was nothing but a material building, it was the house of prayer. It had been set apart for God and had spoken for all these ages of God's presence with his people. Whatever might be the value of its rites and ceremonies it was the outward sign of something above the world. Men were made conscious in this house that God was over them and was with them as a living presence and that they might hold fellowship with him. This was how

Jesus thought of the temple. Some have argued from his action that he approved of ritual worship, others that he condemned it, but considerations of this nature were not in his mind at all. The temple, as he saw it was God's house, witnessing to men that God was in the midst of them and they must serve and trust him. This, in whatever form it might be expressed, was the central fact of religion, and no evil custom must be allowed to obscure it.

It may thus be granted that Jesus never shook off his Judaism. He himself declared that he had come not to destroy the Law but to fulfil it, and it was in that sense that he brought a new religion. He took the beliefs which men had always held and disclosed the truth that lay hidden in them. They were entangled with false ideas which made them ineffectual and his aim was to reach down to those vital principles which lay at the heart of them. So he remained faithful to the old religion. He worshipped in the synagogue, repeating the ancient prayers with his new conception of their meaning. He cherished the scriptures, interpreting them in the light of his deeper knowledge of God. Above all, he shared the reverence which men had ever felt for the temple. For him, as for the others, it was the holy place where God, in some mysterious manner, had his abode, and it was in this conviction that he drove out those who had dared to profane it.

His zeal for this house of God was thus perfectly sincere, and yet at this point we have to reckon with the saying which seems to contradict his act. It is recorded in somewhat different terms by Matthew, Mark and John, but the version in Mark probably comes nearest to what he actually said: "I will destroy this temple which is made with hands, and in three days I will build another, made without hands." * It was chiefly on the ground of this saying that he was accused before the Council and condemned, and in this connection we shall have to consider it later; but it also has an all-important bearing on the general question of his attitude to the temple.

According to the Synoptic writers it was reported to the Council by false witnesses, but this does not mean that Jesus never spoke the words attributed to him. The witnesses were false in so far as they could not agree on the exact words, and everything turned on this in a court of law. Moreover, they had torn the words from their context and quoted them with a malignant purpose. There can be no doubt, however, that Jesus really spoke them. This is confirmed by the very fact that the witnesses disagreed, as they would not have done if they had conspired to invent the incriminating words. John takes for granted that the saying is genuine, and it re-appears in the book of Acts as part of the indictment of Stephen, who had repeated it in his teaching.† We are told also that bystanders at the Cross mocked at Jesus as the man who had boasted that he would destroy the temple and re-build it. Of all the sayings of Jesus this

* Mk. 14:58.
† Ac. 6:14.

is perhaps the best attested. A wish has often been expressed that we had some knowledge of Jesus from sources quite uncoloured by Christian prejudice. It is held that evidence of this kind could be relied on, and might entirely change our idea of what he taught. One saying has come to us directly from his enemies and was selected for the very purpose of proving the case against him. It is in full harmony with all the rest of his recorded teaching, and stands out, the more we ponder it, as one of the grandest of all his sayings.

It appears in the Fourth Gospel as part of the incident of the cleansing of the temple. There were some, we are told, who resented the high-handed act of Jesus and asked him for a sign which would justify his presumption. He said "Destroy this temple and in three days I will re-build it," and the Evangelist explains this as pointing forward to the Resurrection. Such an answer would have been utterly irrelevant, and the aim is clearly to force the saying into connection with the incident. This, as we have seen, cannot be done. At the very moment when he vindicated the holiness of the temple Jesus would not declare that it was only of temporary value and that his purpose was to remove it altogether. Yet the saying must belong to the same general period as the cleansing. It speaks of "this temple," indicating that Jesus had the magnificent building before his eyes. The "false witnesses," too, were obviously reporting what they had heard quite recently. Presumably they were spies of the chief priests who had been set to keep watch on Jesus as he taught in the temple

courts and take note of any compromising words. That
the saying had some relation to the incident is more
than likely. The action of Jesus may have given rise to
a discussion, later in the day or on the day following, as
to the nature and significance of the temple, in the
course of which he would show that it was holy because
it typified the divine presence. In itself, as every one
could see, it was the work of men's hands and was
bound to perish, as everything material must. Yet it
would disappear only to give place to something not
made with hands—to the reality which it foreshadowed,
the true and eternal house of God. Jesus would naturally go on to speak of his own mission. He had come
to hasten the time when the material would be superseded by the spiritual, and this change might be effected
almost at once ("in three days" was the ordinary way of
saying "in a very short time") if the purport of his message was rightly understood. The temple had been fifty
years in building and was still unfinished. He would
make it possible for any true servant of God to worship
him with hardly an interval in a new kind of temple.
It is not hard to see how the saying in its original setting would explain itself, as it evidently did. There is
no sign that it caused the shock and uproar which
would certainly have followed if Jesus had suddenly
told that crowd of pilgrims, gathered from great dis-
tances to do honour to the temple, that he intended to
destroy it. He had made it plain to them what he meant,
and they were in sympathy with him. It was only the
hired informers, waiting to catch him in some un-

guarded utterance, who seized on this one as blasphemous.

Thus the saying, although it did not strictly belong
to the incident, had a real connection with it and was
meant to throw light on its import. Jesus now said in
words what he had implicitly said in his action. He had
purified the temple, not from any sentimental feeling
for a place hallowed by great memories, but because it
made real to men the presence of God. This, for him,
was the significance of the temple, and he wished that
others should be conscious of it as he was himself. The
worldly traffic stood in the way of any true apprehension
of God and must therefore be removed. But if the temple was sacred because of the truth it signified, was it
not itself an obstruction? It is the danger of all symbols
that they come in time to be confused with the reality.
Jeremiah in a former age had warned the people against
a vain trust in the temple for its own sake. Under the
shadow of disaster they had kept repeating "This is the
temple of the Lord," assured that in the mere building
there was a magic power that would save them.* Jesus
also perceived that the temple was obscuring the great
fact which made it holy. It pointed to something beyond itself, and his task was to reveal the substance of
which it was the shadow. "I will destroy this temple
made with hands and will build another, made without
hands." The thought is just the same as in the great
declaration in the Fourth Gospel. "Not in this mountain nor yet in Jerusalem, for the hour cometh and now

* Jer. 7:4.

is when the true worshippers shall worship the Father in spirit and in truth; for the Father seeketh such to worship him." *

Thus there is no contradiction between the saying of Jesus and the action which preceded it. Both of them disclose the same attitude of mind, and they serve to explain one another. Jesus had a profound reverence for the temple and sought to preserve it from sacrilege. But he revered it only for what it represented. Men had tried to declare by this house they had built for him that God, who rules in heaven, is also present on earth, and that without him they could do nothing. This acknowledgement of God was for Jesus the primary condition of human life. The prayer which he taught his disciples begins with the words "Hallowed be thy name." This, he indicates, is the foundation of all else. Your life has no meaning and you can ask for nothing unless you stand in awe of the Holy One who is above this world and yet ever beside you. The temple was the expression in visible form of this reverence for God, and had therefore to be preserved from all contamination. Jesus cleansed it because he realised so intensely what it signified, and this sense of what it stood for also found utterance in his saying that he would destroy and re-build it. He meant that, although it was an earthly house, perishable like all else that is made with hands, it was in substance eternal. Through all changes in outward form the thing expressed by it would become ever clearer and more certain. A temple would rise up when

* Jn. 4:23.

it was fallen in which God would be present in very deed. The saying has a far-reaching import and may be applied to all the human struggle towards higher things. That which is attained is always imperfect and points to something beyond itself. A time comes when the belief or institution which once seemed final is only an obstruction to its own purpose and needs to be destroyed. All that we build has sooner or later to perish, but through this failure of our best efforts we prepare the way for something that will be real and everlasting.

So we must remember this other side of Jesus' attitude to the temple. He saw in it only an earthly house that would disappear, but still he insisted that it should be kept holy. For the sake of what it pointed to he reverenced the building itself, although it was made by men's hands out of material things. The true temple was in some measure present in this visible one. We know from the whole tenor of his teaching that he never drew a sharp line between the material and the spiritual. He taught by means of parables, discerning in common objects and experiences some correspondence with the great principles of the higher life. He believed that through these earthly things God was revealing himself, and that it is sometimes by means of them we can apprehend him best. Our modern effort is to spiritualise religion, by which we mean too often reducing all facts to abstract ideas. The Gospel history itself is turned into a sort of allegory, in which the things that Jesus actually did are of little consequence. All that matters is some vague spiritual meaning which can be extracted from them. This is supposed to mark our advance on previous ages when everything was taken literally. But does it not rather account for the loss of vitality in our religion? If we are to know God as real we must associate him, not with ideas, but with facts, with things that our eyes can see and our hands can handle. That was the nature of Jesus' own religion, and he reverenced the temple for the very reason that it was an earthly house, a visible witness to the presence of God.

Chapter Five

THE MOTIVES FOR THE CLEANSING

It has been too often assumed that Jesus never did anything without a definite purpose. Each of his recorded actions has been analysed from every point of view in order to discover the motive which must have lain behind it. Much of this enquiry tends only to make Jesus an unnatural figure. A man of noble disposition will do brave and generous things unthinkingly, for no other reason than that he cannot help doing them. This was pre-eminently true of Jesus, and when we conceive of him as always acting with some object, however admirable, we deprive him of the very quality which attracts us. His love and goodness were all unconscious. His will was so identified with that of God that he did spontaneously on every occasion what God would have him do.

In his cleansing of the temple, however, we cannot but look for motives. He knew, when he came to Jerusalem, that the whole issue of his life was now to be decided. His enemies were waiting for their opportu-

nity and he could not afford to do anything rashly on
the mere impulse of the moment. Bent as he was on a
great errand he had to consider, in even his slightest
movements, how he could best accomplish it. We know,
too, that his act in the temple was a deliberate one. He
had seen the traffic that was in process but had restrained himself till he had thought the matter over,
and on the day following he made his protest. It is clear
that he did not act in a sudden passion. He had weighed
all circumstances and possible effects and had decided
that in this manner he could best effect his purpose. We
are fully justified in asking what his motives were in
cleansing the temple.

It is seldom that an action is performed from a single
clear-cut motive. Life is complex and when you make
any important decision many factors have to be taken
into account. This is the difficulty we always meet with
when we try to pass a judgment on any human deed. We
see what the man has done, but his possible motives are
so tangled together that we cannot determine whether
we should praise or blame him. He was aiming at a
large end but also at some immediate one—to obtain an
office, to advance his party interests, to defeat his personal enemies. All these motives may be combined in
one apparently simple action. So Jesus in that culmi-
nating week of his life had many urgent problems all
pressing on him together. Along with the great object
of his mission he had to consider the given circumstances, and the hostile forces which had to be overcome. We cannot isolate any one motive for his cleans-

ing of the temple, for there must have been a number, different in character but all combined.

To all appearances his motive was nothing more than to purify the holy place from a grave abuse, but it has seemed to many that since he had long given up the whole conception of ritual worship he can only have viewed the sacrilege as an outsider. A good Protestant may visit a Catholic church and feel indignant if priests or people behave irreverently during the observance of the Mass. We can imagine Jesus as shocked in like manner by the abuse in the temple. Those who worshipped in it professed to think of it as a holy place, and yet they allowed this profanation. For Jesus himself, however, it had ceased to mean what it meant to the people. It cannot have been any zeal for the temple which induced him to risk everything in order to cleanse it.

We have seen, however, that this is a mistaken view. Jesus revered the temple, and this was evident to those who witnessed his action. They were roused by it and supported him, and no man can exert such influence on others unless he is profoundly moved himself. There was no doubt in the people's minds that he was consumed with zeal for the house of God, and his ardour was far greater than they could perceive, for the temple meant much more to him than it did to them. It was the symbol of that presence of God which he realised with the whole force of his being. When we enquire into the motives of his action we must never forget this one which gave significance to all the others. He cleansed the temple because it was indeed, in all that it implied for him, the object of his deepest devotion. Its purity was no side-issue, for he was intent, above all else, on preserving a right attitude to God. To know him as the Holy One, to realise his presence—this for Jesus was the very substance of religion, and it was manifested in the temple.

His action, therefore, was not inconsistent with his message of the Kingdom of God but was an essential part of it. The Kingdom was that new order of things when God alone would reign and all things would be done in accordance with his will. It was now at hand and men must be ready for it and live already as if it were come. If there was no living sense of God, if the thought of him was all confused with earthly things, the message of his coming Kingdom would be meaningless. Men had first to be awakened to the knowledge that God was real and very near to them; and he had appointed this house where they could feel that they stood under his shadow. Religion in all ages has sought a foot-hold in some actual contact with the divine. In ancient Paganism this was sought in a mood of ecstasy in which the worshipper was rapt out of himself and seemed to be lifted into a higher world. In the Middle Ages men clung to sacraments, or tried by mystical contemplation to attain even for a moment the beatific vision. A visit to the temple had a similar value to the pious Israelite. The Psalmist utters his cry, "My soul thirsteth for God, for the living God; when shall I come and appear before God?" His desire will be satisfied when he stands in the temple. "Bring me unto thy holy hill and to thy tabernacle; then will I go unto the altar of God, unto God my exceeding joy." * The temple gave that certainty of God without which no man could truly serve him, and Jesus required that before men sought the Kingdom they should have the full assurance of God. This was the very basis of his religion, and it was in his mind when he cleansed the temple. The house of God must be kept holy. It was only a building made with hands, but it stood for the primary truth which gave meaning to the message of the Kingdom.

There is no need, therefore, to explain the action of Jesus in any vague, allegorical fashion. His fundamental motive when he cleansed the temple was that which he professed it to be. He felt that men could not worship God unless they were conscious of his holiness, and this was impossible so long as his house of prayer was degraded into a place of merchandise. To dishonour it in this manner was to strike at the very root of religion. However else we may account for his action, it must not be forgotten that this was its obvious and its primary meaning. Yet we have also to remember that he performed it at the crisis of his mission, when everything he did must have had some bearing on the great enterprise on which he was engaged. The purpose of a statesman in a time of danger is to win security for his country, but his mind is immediately occupied with the

* Pss. 42-43.

measures he must take in the given circumstances to ensure that end. We have to ask ourselves what were the definite motives of Jesus besides the larger one.

His action may be illustrated, in this respect, by the Pauline Epistles. Paul wrote to the Romans in order to affirm the truth of the Christian message, and his letter has been commonly expounded from this one point of view. But we have now come to see that within this larger purpose there were more specific ones. Paul wrote this Epistle, like all the others, to a particular group of people who were in a special situation, and that must never be left out of sight. Much that is obscure in his thought would be explained if we took his more definite motives into account. This is no less true of the acts and the sayings of Jesus, and particularly so in this incident of the cleansing of the temple. It took place in that momentous week when he was bringing his work to fulfilment, and we have to consider what was his position at that time. Who were his friends and opponents? What were the difficulties in his way? His mind was full of his great purpose but he had to plan the course that he must steer for its achievement.

Two things must have been uppermost in his thoughts when he arrived at Jerusalem. On the one hand, he was now convinced that he was the Messiah. Ever since he had declared himself to his disciples this idea of his Messiahship must have possessed his mind, almost to the exclusion of every other. God had called him to be the Messiah and henceforth he must act in this capacity.

There can be little doubt that it was under stress of the
Messianic conviction he went up to Jerusalem. It was
there that he must reveal himself; something would
happen there which would justify his claim and bring
his Messianic work to its fulfilment. We may safely regard his act in the temple as connected in some manner
with his knowledge that he was no other than the Messiah. On the other hand, while he realised his supreme
office he was aware of a mounting opposition. For some
time past he had been under constant attack, and it was
now apparent that his life was in danger. With this
knowledge he was venturing into the city in which the
power of his enemies was concentrated. There may have
been other conditions by which his movements were
determined during that final week, but of these two we
can be certain. He knew that he was encountering a
fearful peril, and in the face of it he was called on to
assert his claim to be the promised Messiah.

There might seem to be little relation between his
sense of a supreme mission and his action in the temple.
He had come to offer himself as the Messiah, and all
that he did was to drive out some cattle-dealers, tres-
passing in the temple court. We cannot but feel that
this was an anti-climax, and it has been maintained that
for the time being he forgot himself. Carried away by a
sudden indignation he made much of a very trifling
matter, never thinking of his mission or of the majesty
that should belong to it. But those who witnessed his
act and reflected on it would see it differently. According to the current belief, one of the functions of the

Messiah would be the correction of all errors in worship. In the regulations laid down in the Mosaic law many things were obscure and doubtful, and even the ablest Rabbis were at variance in their interpretations. It had been agreed that when any rule of the Law could be understood in several ways the usual custom should be allowed to stand, with the proviso added, "Until the Messiah comes." This was a formula constantly employed in Jewish religion, and it finds a place in the conversation of Jesus with the woman of Samaria. She admits that the question of the true place of worship is an open one and says "When the Messiah comes he will order all things." * As the people watched the cleansing of the temple it must have occurred to many that this was just the kind of action expected of the Messiah. We know that by this time Jesus had excited a wide-spread curiosity, and that there were many guesses as to who he might be. Some thought he was John the Baptist re-appearing, some that he was Elijah who was to return in the latter days, some that he was a new prophet or one of the ancient ones sent back to earth.† The rumour that he was Messiah had already sprung up and had doubtless reached Jerusalem. At least some of those who watched him would tell themselves that he was acting as the Messiah would do, and we can believe that Jesus meant to awaken this surmise. He purposely performed an act which would indicate his Messianic calling.

* Jn. 4:25.
† Mk. 8:28.

The cleansing of the temple may thus be regarded as the nearest approach he ever made to an open proclamation. His silence on the cardinal matter of his Messiahship has been fixed on by many modern writers as the chief problem in the Gospel history. If he believed himself to be the Messiah why did he never declare it? The theory has been put forward that the claim was only made for him by his disciples after his death. On his own part, he never professed to be more than a prophet, but his followers, in their reverence for him, insisted that he had been the very Messiah. In answer to the difficulty that he had never made such a claim they held that he had kept it a secret, divulging it only to an inner circle. On many grounds this theory may be set aside, and it will be necessary at a later stage to consider the nature of his Messianic conception. At present we are concerned only with his apparent silence. Why was it that he was content merely to suggest, by such an act as his cleansing of the temple, that he was clothed with Messianic power? It may be that he intended to follow up his act by some definite announcement for which no opportunity was given him but of this there is no evidence. Most probably he never meant to declare himself in formal words. It was not his way to strive and cry and make his voice heard in the streets. He never tried to force himself on public notice but believed that light would shine by its own power, and that truth spoken in an inner chamber would some day be shouted from the house-tops. He may well have felt that a statement in words, however confidently made, would carry

no conviction. Many had already laid claim to Messiahship, but no one had believed them except crazy fanatics
like themselves. Nothing can really speak but actions,
and Jesus was satisfied to act like the Messiah, and leave
men to form their own judgment of who he must be. It
is significant that even at Caesarea Philippi he made no
statement of his own but only drew a confession from
his disciples. They had been watching and hearing him
all this time; what impression had he made on them?
"Who do you say that I am?" If his actions were not self-
evidently those of the Messiah no assertion he could
make would be worth anything. It was in this manner,
we may assume, that he wished to declare himself at
Jerusalem. He would do the works of the Messiah, and
they would speak for him. And in all times since his
claim has been acknowledged, not on the ground of his
own assertion, but because men have heard him for
themselves and know that this is indeed the Christ, the
Saviour of the world.*

In cleansing the temple, then, he declared his Messiahship by a significant act, and also made it evident
that his function was a religious one. For the people
generally the Messiah was the future king who would
deliver Israel. He would beat down all enemies and rule
justly and gloriously over a nation to which all others
would be subject. Jesus was well aware that this was
how his claim would be interpreted and wished to make
it clear from the first that he was not a Messiah in any
political sense. If he had begun his work in Jerusalem

* Jn. 4:42.

by denouncing some flagrant wrong on the part of governors or judges or the privileged classes he would have marked himself out as an agitator in this world's affairs. Any claim that he made to be the Messiah would henceforth be regarded in this light. So the evil against which he protested was one that was wholly concerned with religion. He stood in the house of God and declared, in right of his Messiahship, that it must be kept holy. By this act he disowned all those false ideas which had grown up in the popular mind around the name of Messiah. In claiming the office he identified it at the same time with pure religion. He had nothing to do with political ambitions. It was not the cause of Israel which he had at heart but only the cause of God, which had its visible expression in the temple.

At this point, however, we can discern the more specific motive which lay behind the action. The temple with all that it signified was in charge of the hereditary priests. It was they who offered the daily prayers and sacrifices, and the high-priest once a year entered the holy of holies to renew the covenant between God and his people. The religion of Israel was consummated in that solemn moment when the nation, in the person of its high-priest, stood face to face with God and all the priests, in their different degrees, had part in his sublime office. How had they discharged their trust? They had allowed the temple, where God met with his people, to be used as a market-place. Merchants and money-

changers were brawling in the very vestibule to that
mysterious sanctuary where God revealed himself.

It cannot be doubted that Jesus intended by his act to
rebuke the priesthood, and especially the chief priests
who controlled the others. They knew of the unholy
traffic and permitted it. They did so, although this is not
directly stated, for purposes of gain. For the defilement
of the temple they were responsible, and it would be
evident to all the onlookers that the protest of Jesus was
aimed at them. Others had acquiesced in the evil custom
because it was sanctioned by those venerated men, but
when Jesus spoke out the public conscience was awakened. It was plainly he, and not the official priests, who
had a true zeal for the house of God.

He thus attacked the priestly authorities, but why did
he do it in that open manner at that particular time? All
through his previous ministry he had carefully avoided
any needless provocation of those who differed from
him, and he owed it to this that he had been able to
work so long unmolested. At any moment by a single
rash word he might have played into the hands of his
enemies, but he had always been guarded and circum-
spect. Traps were cunningly laid for him but he had
seen them in time and had stepped aside. He had been
asked dangerous questions and had answered them in
such a way that no one could find fault. The Gospels are
full of instances of this marvellous discretion which
made it possible for Jesus to walk unharmed amidst
snares and pit-falls. Yet in those closing days he seems

to have thrown all prudence to the winds. He knew that in Jerusalem the chief priests were all-powerful and that he could effect nothing if they took sides against him; but his very first act was to provoke them in a manner they could not overlook. He went out of his way to do so, for in view of the far graver matters he had at heart he need not have interfered with arrangements of the temple. Even if he had felt it imperative that an abuse should cease he might have achieved his end without a direct affront to the high officers. Yet he performed an act which could have no other consequence than to enrage the very men who had most power to injure him. He did this, not on a sudden impulse of anger, but after a night's deliberation.

So it has appeared to many that his cleansing of the temple was the height of folly. They deny that it happened or assume that at this point there is some confusion in the record. It may have been that Jesus made a protest of some kind but the Gospel account of the incident may be set aside as incredible. To accept it is to hold Jesus himself responsible for the events that led to his death. He wantonly stirred up the hostility of the chief priests, and against their opposition, in the city which they ruled, his cause was hopeless. Can it be believed that of his own initiative he brought them into the field against him and thereby sealed his doom?

Such argument, however, rests on the assumption that hitherto the priests had not concerned themselves about Jesus, and it is true that we hear nothing of their interference in the course of the Galilean ministry. Their place was in Jerusalem, and Jesus could not come into direct contact with them. As official magistrates they had no jurisdiction in Galilee, and their meddling with local affairs would have been resented. But it does not follow that they stood entirely aloof from the new movement. Such indifference was impossible, for they were accountable to Rome for the peace of the country, and Jesus was clearly gaining an influence which might make him the leader of a revolt. They were responsible, too, for the national religion. It was now identified with the observance of the Law, but the Law was anchored to the temple, which was the very house of God and gave meaning and reality to the requirements of the Law. It is sometimes assumed that the priestly Council which passed judgment on Jesus took no account of his religious teaching, but this is a profound mistake. Whatever might be their worldly interests the chief priests could never forget that their office was primarily a religious one. They could not but fear that the work of Jesus would bring disaster to the religion of which they were the appointed guardians. It was only a short time afterwards that the Council sent out its delegates, of whom Saul of Tarsus was one, to warn all synagogues within Palestine and beyond it against the new Christian beliefs. In Jesus' life-time the chief priests, as the representatives of the true faith, would feel the same obligation.

We may be sure, then, that almost from the first they were keenly alive to all that was happening in Galilee. A movement had begun in that excitable province which might soon convulse the whole country. It was impossible that the acknowledged leaders in all that concerned the welfare of Israel should do nothing while multitudes from every quarter were acclaiming the new prophet. They must have watched his progress with the deepest anxiety. They must have tried by every means they could to thwart his mission. But for many reasons they could not attack him openly. In Galilee they had no official power. They wished to avoid any conflict with the people, who were manifestly on the side of Jesus. Their settled practice, too, was to gain their ends by indirect methods, and it was doubtless in this manner that they worked against Jesus. Remaining themselves in the background, they set in motion various forces which would destroy his influence and perhaps effect his death. We have seen reason to believe that all through the Galilean period they were behind the opposition to Jesus. It is the undoubted fact that the men who finally compassed his death were the chief priests. It was they who had him arrested and tried and sentenced, and their animosity must have been deeply rooted and of long standing. A great crime is seldom committed hastily. Even when it seems to be the outcome of sudden passion it can be traced back to hatreds and jealousies which have been secretly active perhaps for years. As Jesus himself said, wicked deeds come from the heart and are only the manifestations of what has there been hidden. This was true, we may be sure, of the men who crucified Jesus. They had been contemplating his death before they ever saw him and were ready as soon as the chance was offered them to carry out their designs.

Here, then, we can perceive a motive for the cleansing of the temple. This affront to the chief priests at the very outset of his work in Jerusalem might seem to be sheer madness on the part of Jesus. He had always kept clear of quarrels which might distract him from his high purpose, and now he provoked one himself. It turned on a matter of little importance which did not much concern him, and the men whose enmity he excited were those he most needed to conciliate. Of his own accord they brought down on him the anger of the revered heads of the national religion, who were also the administrators of justice.

The imprudence of his action must have been more evident to himself than it can be to us, and he must have had some potent reason for it. There is only one which can adequately meet the facts. He was aware that all along the chief priests had been his real adversaries. They had been responsible for all the opposition but had thus far been careful to conceal themselves and to attack him by the hands of others. It was necessary that they should be forced into the open. Until they disclosed themselves he was only fighting against shadows and nothing that he did would be of much avail. Now that he was making his final venture he must know definitely where he stood. There must be an end to this intriguing and undermining, and his enemies must declare themselves and meet him face to face. The danger that threatened him might become even greater than it

was before, but he would no longer be fighting in the
dark. This, we can hardly doubt, was one of his reasons,
and perhaps the chief one, for making his journey to
Jerusalem. He had become certain that the antagonism
he had to reckon with was that of the priests, and it was
necessary that he should encounter them in their citadel.
Tremendous issues were in the balance, and they had
to be decided in the light of day.

An incident is preserved in Luke's Gospel which helps
us to realise the position of Jesus during the later part
of his ministry.* He was warned by friendly Pharisees
that Herod had planned to kill him, and it was probably
owing to this timely warning that he withdrew from
Galilee into the North. But the answer he made on that
occasion is highly significant. "Go and tell that fox—that
I must work to-day and to-morrow and the day following, for it cannot be that a prophet should perish out of
Jerusalem." He was prepared for death, and knew that
it was coming, but he was resolved that he would not
be murdered in some secret place at the whim of a petty
tyrant. He would die as the prophets had done in the
capital of the nation with the world looking on. It was
the tragedy of his life that he knew himself to be encom-
passed with hidden enemies. He was conscious that even
among his immediate disciples there was a traitor, and
probably till the very moment of the betrayal he could
not tell for certain which of them it might be. To know
that you are in deadly peril and yet to be ignorant of
what it is and from what quarter it may fall on you—

* Lk. 13:31-33.

this, of all conditions of mind, is the most unnerving.
Jesus, in the later period, found himself in that position. He longed to break through that web of secret
malice which was being woven around him. Let his
enemies reveal themselves and he would know how to
meet them. They might do their worst but anything
would be better than this walking in darkness amidst
hidden dangers.

We can thus see a meaning in that action of Jesus
which seems at first sight so contrary to the prudence
which had hitherto guided him. He must have seen that
he would incense the very men whom it was his interest
to keep quiet, but this was his intention. In the most
pointed way he could think of he threw down a challenge to the chief priests. These were his enemies but
they had always worked secretly in the background. He
was determined that they should come forward in their
own persons and confront him. The challenge he offered
them was one they could not possibly decline. They
were the guardians of the temple and on this they depended for their authority and for their very existence,
and he now told them, in a manner which could not be
mistaken, that they had been unfaithful to their trust.
They had permitted sacrilege in this house of God
which it was their one duty to keep holy. He thus attacked them at the point where they were most sensitive,
and he did this publicly during the solemn festival
where they officiated in all their glory. They could not
allow an act of this kind to pass unnoticed. Their plan
had no doubt been to continue their secret policy and

get him removed by other agents without any gesture of
their own which might compromise them. Jesus had
decided to make this impossible. His act was like the
blow by which in old days the man who had been
wronged compelled his enemy to meet him, sword in
hand. The priestly officials had no choice but to accept
his challenge. They heard of it, Mark tells us, and immediately consulted together as to how they might destroy
him.*

Three different motives can thus be distinguished in
Jesus' cleansing of the temple. There was first his indignation when he saw the holy place profaned. He did not
pretend this zeal for the temple, nor was it due to a
mere sentiment, springing from old memories and asso-
ciations. He reverenced the earthly building because it
stood for the eternal fact that God was over the world
and men had access to him. Again, he wished to assert
his own Messiahship. God had appointed him to this
office, and he had the right to act in the name of God.
He was Lord of the temple and his authority in all that
concerned it had to be accepted as the final one. Once
more, he meant by his action to force his enemies out
of their hiding-places. It was the chief priests who had
been seeking by crafty methods to frustrate his work
and who would do their utmost to crush him now that
he had come within their reach. He would at least make
sure that the conflict would be an open one. Those
secret enemies must unmask themselves, and he offered

* Mk. 11:18.

them a defiance which they could not refuse to answer. His cause had now to be decided and the adversaries must stand face to face.

The three motives may seem to have little relation to each other but it is not difficult to see how they blended in the mind of Jesus and found their outcome in the one act. He was shocked by the profanation of the temple and desired to purify it, but he could do so only by asserting his authority as the Messiah. This, he knew, would involve him in conflict with the religious leaders, but since they were already his enemies he resolved to challenge them. Most probably he was not himself aware of any complexity in his motives. He had come to Jerusalem with his heart set on one great purpose and was conscious at the same time of the opposition he would have to encounter. It was necessary that at the very outset he should perform an act which would at once declare his purpose and call forth the opposing forces. He decided after full deliberation that he could express everything that was in his mind by this one act of cleansing the temple.

His cardinal motive was doubtless that which he himself indicated by the words which accompanied his act. He saw in the temple the house of prayer for all nations —the place in which men could realise God's presence and make their approach to him. His own message was grounded in the conviction which this building expressed in visible form; that God is the great reality, and that men must live for him and serve him. But as the temple spoke to him of God it reminded him also

that he was himself the Messiah, whose office it was
act for God and fulfil his purposes with men. Ever sinc
his momentous confession to the disciples this sense of
his Messiahship had taken full possession of him and
had determined everything that he thought and did. His
cleansing of the temple must be regarded as a definite
Messianic act. Before we can understand it in this light
we need to consider what he meant when he claimed to
be the Messiah. This is the question on which all the
problems in his history must finally converge.

Chapter Six

THE MESSIANIC CLAIM

One thing stands out above all others in Jesus' cleansing of the temple. He did not argue or remonstrate but commanded. He bade the traffickers depart because he so willed it, and he took for granted that his will had to be obeyed. This side of his action is emphasised in the Fourth Gospel by the addition that he used a scourge to drive out the evil-doers. For many reasons this is incredible, but it brings out the fact that his word had a compulsive power to which those who heard him had to submit. They knew the Master of the house, whose orders could not be questioned. At the moment they and all the onlookers were taken by surprise and could only bow to the superior will; but when the incident was over they began to wonder why they had not resisted. "By what authority doest thou these things, and who gave thee this authority?" This was the point on which all controversy turned during the days that followed. Judaism was a religion which rested on authority —the requirements of the Law, of the scriptures, of long-

established custom. Everything was strictly ordained,
and there could be no departure from the set rule even
in the most trivial details. Jesus had acted on some new
kind of authority, or rather had made himself an authority which superseded all the others. This was an
offence which could not be forgiven and for which he
was at last put to death.

The authority by which he cleansed the temple was
that of the Messiah. He performed just the type of action which was expected of the Messiah, the deputy of
God who would correct all disorders of worship and
ensure that God's name should be duly hallowed. He
clearly intended that those who witnessed his act should
so understand it, and infer that he was no other than
the promised Messiah. But a question of far-reaching
importance here arises. A king possesses authority in
virtue of a true hereditary claim. If there is some flaw
in his descent his title is not valid, and his people can
feel free to throw off their loyalty. In much the same
way the authority of Jesus has sometimes been chal-
lenged. He claimed to be the Messiah, but could he
really make out his title? Had he the formal credentials
by which men were to know the Messiah when he came?
If he had no right to the title which he assumed, his
authority must fall to the ground.

It cannot be denied that when the Messianic claim is
placed at the centre our Christian belief in Jesus lies
open to serious attack. Jewish opponents contended
from the first that he was not the Messiah foretold in
scripture and were able to point to many discrepancies

between his history and the prophetic hopes. They could argue that since he was plainly not the expected Messiah the religion based on his claim was nothing but a delusion. In modern times the question has been approached from other points of view. Doubts have been raised as to whether he ever claimed to be the Messiah, or it is maintained that if he did so, he did not commit himself to anything. The Messiah was only an imaginary figure. Men have dreamed in all ages of what would happen in the future, and their speculations turned in ancient times on a wonderful being who would some day appear and renew all things by a divine power. There can be no argument as to whether Jesus was or was not the Messiah, since this name was never meant to denote a real Personality. In ways like this the attempt is made to dissociate the work of Jesus from the Messianic idea, and it is justified, in some measure, by the New Testament writings themselves. As we read the Epistles of Paul we cannot but feel that he has moved away from the traditional conception and is seeking to interpret it in a larger sense. When he speaks of Jesus as the Christ he does not think of ancient prophecies but of a divine nature inherent in Jesus. He was the Lord, the Son of God, the Redeemer. Men must own his sovereignty because they inwardly respond to his revelation of God. The title Messiah, for Paul and the later New Testament teachers, becomes only another name for Jesus himself.

It cannot be doubted, however, that Jesus thought of the prophets as inspired men who were vouchsafed a

vision of the future, and saw an actual Person who
would arise in the latter days and fulfil the purpose of
God. It was borne in upon him that he was himself that
Messiah. He struggled against his conviction, which imposed a burden on him that seemed beyond his strength.
But it forced itself on him with an irresistible power
and at last he acknowledged to his disciples that he was
the Messiah who had been foretold. Yet while he accepted the prophecies he did not do so blindly. It is
very noticeable that all through his teaching there is a
critical element in his reverence for the scriptures.
Never doubting that they contain the word of God he
yet compares and judges them, and sets one inspired
text above another. This is his attitude to the Messianic
predictions. He cannot take them in just their literal
sense, but feels that they must be qualified and eluci-
dated. Those holy men beheld the Messiah, but they
saw him from a distance and through a mist. The reality
would in many ways be different from the forecast. It
has sometimes been assumed that Jesus was fettered by
the Messianic beliefs. He had a model set before him
which he was obliged to copy, and was thus constrained
to courses of action which he would not himself have
chosen. This, however, is contrary to all our knowledge
of Jesus, who never allowed his own judgment to be
over-ridden by any theory or tradition. His nature was
such that he could not move freely in grooves prepared
for him but had always to be himself.

One may take as an example the contrast between
him and his fore-runner John the Baptist. John came

forward as a prophet, and this was indeed his calling, but he felt it necessary to enact the part. The ancient prophets had marked themselves out by a peculiar dress and mode of living. They had dwelt aloof from the people and delivered their messages in a given form of impressive language. John took care in all these respects to imitate them so that men should know at once that a new prophet had appeared. Jesus also was conscious of the prophetic impulse, but he came eating and drinking, moved freely among his fellow-men, spoke to them in words of everyday life. He was bound by no ancient precedents but did his prophetic work in the manner that was natural to himself. It was thus, too, that he obeyed his call to be the Messiah. Instead of taking his directions from any forecast of how the Messiah would be required to act he kept true to his own insight into the will of God, although it differed essentially from the old anticipations. If he was the Messiah, it was for himself to determine how he would accomplish his Messianic task.

We have thus to reckon with a free attitude on the part of Jesus. He never questioned that the prophets were right in their vision of a Messiah, and was convinced that he and no other was the Messiah to whom they had pointed. But he realised that they had seen imperfectly. Looking again with his own eyes he perceived where they had been mistaken. The Messiah with whom he identified himself was not he who had been described by the ancient seers but one who answered to

his own conception of what the true messenger of God
must be.

It may here be observed that much of the modern
enquiry into the life and thought of Jesus is based on a
cardinal error. Attention has been rightly fixed on the
historical conditions under which he worked and on
all that he took over from teachers before him. It is
shown that there is hardly one of his sayings for which
some parallel cannot be found in earlier Jewish literature. His main conceptions are those of the Old Testament. He repeats maxims of the Rabbis almost in the
same words. His visions of the future have their counter-
parts in the apocalyptic books. So from all this it has
been inferred that he gave little that was distinctively
new. His religion as a whole was simply the higher Judaism of his time, more ably presented and stripped of
the useless wrappings that encumbered it. But while he
is thus placed in his historical surroundings he himself
is left out of account. The old ideas, as he appre-
hended them, were all transformed. He put something
into them, out of his own personality and his own
knowledge of God, which made all the difference. Nothing is more misleading than to take any saying of Jesus
and construe it in terms of something like it which had
been said by a teacher before him. The modern astron-
omer has largely borrowed the language of the old star-
gazers who believed that all the heavenly bodies moved
round the earth, but we should make little of their text-
books if we read them with just the ancient ideas in our
minds. The new interpretation is the only thing that

matters, and this is equally true of the words of Jesus. We must always ask ourselves first of all what he himself intended by them. It is interesting to learn how they had been understood previously and sometimes this may throw a light on his own thought. But these earlier meanings must not be confounded with the truth he is seeking to convey. He looked at all things from a new point of view, and it is his own mind that we wish to know. This is true in a supreme degree of his Messianic claim. What was its meaning for himself? The title of Messiah had been understood in various ways from the time of the prophets onward, and with many of the hopes and beliefs which had gathered around it he was in little sympathy. He had evidently come to interpret it in a manner of his own, and our concern is not with the earlier anticipations but with the new meaning which that name of Messiah had for Jesus.

It may fairly be asked why he thought it necessary to assume a title which was associated in the general mind with so many ideas which were alien to his own conviction. By calling himself Messiah he was bound to arouse false expectations and to obscure the real nature of his work. Of this he was fully conscious, and here we may find one reason why he made no public proclamation. Might it not have been better if he had left the old prophecies alone and chosen some new title which would have expressed clearly what he knew himself to be? Yet he clung to that name of the Messiah. He was certain that it was he to whom the prophets had looked forward, and was prepared to die, if need be, in defence of his claim. It may indeed seem strange that while he was dissatisfied with the old Messianic idea and felt that in many respects it was mistaken, he yet made it the corner-stone of his whole mission. But he looked beneath the forms in which it had expressed itself to its essential meaning. The prophets had spoken of one who would act in the power of God, who would reveal his will and establish his Kingdom. Their vision had been imperfect but Jesus could not doubt that they were trying to describe the work to which he himself was called. He could be no other than the Messiah who was to come. His attitude to the traditional Messianic hope was much the same as his attitude to the temple. In the one as in the other he grasped the reality through the symbol. The temple was an earthly building but it represented the fact of God's presence. The hope for the Messiah had allied itself with worldly desires and national ambitions, but at the heart of it lay the highest aspirations of man's nature. A day was to come when the true leader would appear and bring the world into that way of life which it had been vainly seeking. Men were looking for this Messiah who would make possible the reign of God.

In another way the prophetic forecasts had value for Jesus. They gave him the inward support without which he could not have found strength to bear up under his tremendous task. One thing has always been necessary to the man who performs a work which might seem utterly beyond him. He must feel that it has not been thrown on him by way of accident but that he has been predestined to it. He is following a path which has been marked out for him, and he cannot choose but walk in it. Paul declares his conviction that God had separated him from his mother's womb to be the Apostle to the Gentiles,* and in the life of every supremely great man we can discern this same sense of obedience to a mission which has been ordained. Jesus could believe that his coming had been prophesied. Ages before he was born it had been decreed that he should do this work which lay before him. He could thus assure himself, in the face of every danger, that he was an instrument in the hand of God.

When we speak, therefore, of the Messianic claim of Jesus two things have always to be distinguished. On the one hand, he had behind him the traditional hope of the Messiah. The prophets had foretold a mighty one who would be clothed with the Spirit and subdue all enemies and bring peace and deliverance. Confident that God had ordained him to fulfil his purposes Jesus identified himself with the expected Messiah. But his sense of a divine commission, while it was fortified by the ancient forecasts, was not dependent on them. There was something in his own nature which impelled him to act for God, and his life would have taken much the same course although he had known nothing of the prophecies. In many ways he was out of sympathy with them, for they rested on conceptions of God's Kingdom and the manner of its coming which were different from his own. When he finally accepted them and applied them to himself he read a new meaning into them. In-

* Gal. 1:15.

stead of conforming his action to the Messianic idea he took that idea and brought it into harmony with his own sense of what God required of him. This insight of his own was always primary with him. He claimed to be the Messiah but such a Messiah as would truly accomplish the will of God.

It is with this fact in mind that we must understand the authority of Jesus. The church has too often assumed that it rested on his office, like that of a king whose word must be obeyed because he is the king. Jesus was the Messiah, divinely appointed to lay his commands on men. His judgments must never be questioned, since he holds a sovereignty from which there can be no appeal. But his authority was not of this official kind. He indeed spoke as the Messiah but his Messiahship was not a position which he happened to occupy, and to which his title, in the view of many, is somewhat doubtful. He possessed it in virtue of the perfect agreement of his will with that will of God which is the ultimate law. He made this apparent in his cleansing of the temple. By that action he claimed an authority superior to that of the acknowledged rulers of the holy place. He intended also that by his action men should know him to be the Messiah. But he took care that his command should not appear to be a mere arbitrary one. While he uttered it he appealed to the conscience of the people, reminding them of what the scriptures had said, awakening their own instinctive sense of how God ought to be worshipped. He was Messiah, not because some divine decree had made him so, but because his mind was fully at one with that of God. He rested his title on this conviction that he knew God as no other had done and gave expression to his will.

It was only in the later part of his ministry that he asserted his Messiahship, but from the outset he was conscious that he had authority. The sick were brought to him and he never doubted that his word and touch would have healing power. When he called on men to follow him he expected them to obey. He confronted old beliefs and customs with his "I say unto you"— assured that his judgment was the final one. It was this note of authority in all his sayings and actions which impressed the people, friends and enemies alike. Here was one who had no need to argue, and whose word was equal to a command. The centurion compared him to a supreme officer who had only to issue his orders, and Jesus commended the faith of this Gentile who had rightly judged him. He was himself aware that he was invested with this power to bend other men to his will.

The sense of authority was thus present in him long before he made any definite Messianic claim. It was inherent in his nature and was not dependent on some office which had been conferred on him. His belief that he was the Messiah grew out of that prior conviction that he was speaking for God, and when he assumed the Messianic title it was still on that conviction that he rested his authority. The title had no meaning for him

apart from that. We are told that during the controversies at Jerusalem he raised the question, "Why say
the scribes that the Messiah will be the son of David?"
Then he quoted the psalm in which David speaks of the
Messiah with adoration, and made his comment, "David
himself calleth him his Lord; how is he then his son?" *
The passage is certainly authentic, for the later church
would never have attributed a saying to Jesus in which
he seemed to deny his descent from David, and thereby
his right to be the Messiah of prophecy. But however
else the saying is to be explained it appears to indicate
plainly that Jesus put aside the traditional Messianic
ideas. For him the greatness of the Messiah would be
altogether different in character from that of David. He
would owe his appointment to God alone. He would
not derive his power from any official position but
simply from the fact that he spoke for God and that
God was working through him. It was this Messiah that
Jesus knew himself to be.

Another of his sayings in that debate which followed
the cleansing of the temple is highly significant.† He
was asked directly "By what authority doest thou these
things, and who gave thee this authority?" He under-
took to answer this question on condition that the
priests and elders who asked it would answer a question
of his own: "What was the authority of John the Baptist?" They refused to say, fearing that however they
answered they might accuse themselves, and Jesus also

* Mk. 12:35-37.
† Mk. 11:27-33.

withheld his answer. If only they had accepted his offer he would have thrown light on many problems which now baffle us. Yet in some measure we can infer from his silence what was in his mind. John had an authority which could not be disputed, but it was not connected with any formal office, for he held none. He was only a solitary voice. Nevertheless he spoke for God, and the power of God was with him and could not be resisted. Jesus was conscious that his own authority was of that order. It could not be defined in terms of any formula or tradition. It resided in himself and in the harmony of his will with that of God.

It is true, then, that Jesus claimed to be the Messiah, but the main question must always be, "How did he conceive of the Messiah?" He took the name from scripture and tradition. He also took over the fundamental idea of one who would appear in the latter days and bring the promises of God to fulfilment. But to all previous thought of the Messiah he owed only a few suggestions, and we must not interpret his claim, as many modern writers are prone to do, from the expectations which were current in his time. He had his own conception of the Messiah, and he derived it, not from prophecy or tradition, but from a source within him. The Messiah whom he had in mind would reveal the true nature of God. He would be in sympathy with men and would raise the fallen and bring comfort to the poor and afflicted. He would create a new order of things, not for one nation, but for all mankind. It is not too much to say that the old Messianic idea was for Jesus little more than the block of marble which grew into form and meaning under the sculptor's hands.

It was in this light that Paul understood the Messiahship of Jesus. He values the title only for what Jesus had put into it by his teaching and his death. Paul was apparently the first to speak of "Jesus Christ"—making the official name inseparable from the personal one. He thus indicates, perhaps unconsciously, his attitude of mind. He was familiar with the Jewish Messianic theories, and their influence is apparent in some aspects of his thinking. But his whole idea of the Messiah has been transformed by his knowledge of how Jesus lived and died. In the approved tradition there was no place for the Cross. It was Jesus himself who had introduced this strange element, and Paul's faith was centred on that fact about him which was most in conflict with the ancient hope. He believed in the Messiah, but in the "Jesus Messiah"; not the one foretold by the prophets but this other who had been realised in Jesus.

Thus, while declaring himself the Messiah, Jesus gave a new significance to the title, and he indicated this by his action in the temple. The Messiah whom men expected was a glorious king who would deliver Israel from the foreign yoke and inaugurate an age of prosperity. Jesus made it clear that his work as Messiah was to bring men into a right relation to God. The temple was God's house, and it must be kept holy. If the sense of God was contaminated by worldly interests there could be no true worship, no true life, for everything else depends on how we think of God. Jesus asserted his tremendous claim by driving some cattle-dealers out of a sacred building, and on the face of it this may appear almost ludicrous. Yet by so acting he discarded all the old ideas of Messiahship. He declared that the primary need of men was to be made alive to the presence of God. This was the kind of work the Messiah would do, and it was the very greatest.

He claimed, then, that he had himself been chosen to establish the right relation between God and men. He had the knowledge of what God requires. He had a consuming zeal for God's house—for the cause of God in this world. It was this consciousness that he stood for God which gave him his authority. He expressed it by calling himself the Messiah, but the title as he assumed it did not denote a mere office, his right to which might be disputed. He was the Messiah in virtue of what he was, in his own Person. He knew that he thought as God did. His one aim was to fulfil God's purposes. It mattered little whether he answered at all points to that Coming One whom prophets had seen in vision. God had appointed him to the supreme task and he must be the Messiah.

Jesus thus summed up his message in the name he took over from the old tradition. It came to signify his religion, and his followers were known as the Christians, that is, the people who believed in the Messiah. The earliest preaching all centred on this one theme, "Let all the house of Israel know assuredly that God hath made this Jesus whom ye have crucified Lord and Mes-

siah." * In all times since, the church has based its faith
on this primary conviction that Jesus was the Messiah,
and therefore the sovereign Lord. Yet in one sense this
is a wrong understanding of his claim. He did not call
on men to believe in him on the ground of his Messiahship. They were to realise, first of all, that he spoke for
God, that he brought a message to which all that was
divine in their own nature responded. Conscious of this,
they were to acknowledge him as the Messiah. This title
had been devised by holy men in the past to express all
that they could imagine as highest. Jesus had given reality to it. In his own life he perfectly manifested the will
of God, and it is for this reason that we still think of
him as the Messiah. It matters little whether he literally
fulfilled the old predictions, which were only guesses at
the best. His life stands out forever as that before which
we must bow with reverence, and beyond which we can
conceive of nothing higher. In this sense he was the
Messiah who should come, and we cannot look for another.

* Ac. 2:36.

Chapter Seven

THE SEQUEL TO THE CLEANSING

The action of Jesus was a challenge to the temple authorities, and Mark tells us that it was answered immediately: "and the chief priests and scribes heard of it and sought how they might destroy him, for they feared him, for all the multitude were astonished at his teaching." * The different parts of this statement do not seem to hang together, but the connection becomes clear when the word "how" is emphasised. It was not the removal of Jesus that was in question but the manner in which it might be effected. The people were on his side, for his teaching had greatly impressed them. His influence over them was more apparent than ever from the support they had just given him in his audacious act. Any attempt to proceed against him openly would be certain to raise a tumult, and some plan had to be devised whereby he might be secretly arrested and brought to judgment.

It is here that we find the explanation of much that is

* Mk. 11:18.

perplexing in the events that follow. Why was Jesus left for some time unmolested? Why was it necessary that he should be seized by treachery and tried in the dark hours? The answer is that his enemies had to guard against the multitude. They could not feel secure until they were able to shift the responsibility to the Roman power. It has been a tragic error, resulting in ages of senseless persecution, which has laid the guilt of the death of Jesus on the Jewish people. The truth is that the Jews as a people were in sympathy with him, and never more so than in the closing days. Their friendliness was his one defence, and the difficulty of his enemies was to effect their purpose in spite of them and without their knowledge. These enemies were no doubt Jews but they were only a small official group, and their position must not be confounded with that of the nation as a whole.

The brief notice in Mark's Gospel is significant in another way. It indicates that the chief priests were already resolved on Jesus' death, and were only in doubt as to the safest means of ensuring it. The view has sometimes been held that until now they had known little or nothing about Jesus, or had regarded him as harmless. His action in the temple had forced him upon their notice and roused them to anger. They now perceived that he was a dangerous man, and decided at a hurried meeting that he must die. His cleansing of the temple has thus been fixed on as the direct cause of his condemnation. But apparently it was never mentioned at his trial, and the hostility of the priesthood had a much deeper root

than in that particular incident. Jesus was aware when
he set out for Jerusalem that he was now to face his real
enemies. Even when he was pursuing his work in Galilee he knew that he would have to suffer many things
and perish like the prophets before him, and it was only
from the high authorities of the nation that he could
expect such a doom. His cleansing of the temple was
not the cause but only the occasion of the struggle
which now began. There had been meetings, long before
that decisive one, at which the chief priests had discussed
him and settled among themselves that he must be removed. His latest act had only made it clear to them
that they could delay no longer. He had openly defied
them, and they had now to consider what measures they
should take to effect his speedy death.

It is evident from many signs that the final attack on
Jesus was not sudden and accidental. The opposition to
him was of long standing and we may believe that some
general plan for his destruction had already been drawn
up and was only waiting to be carried out in detail. For
one thing, there is the undoubted fact that he was fully
conscious of his danger. He had reason to know, when
he went to Jerusalem, that he was venturing into the
midst of deadly enemies. He must have grown aware of
this from all that he had observed and suspected in the
course of his work in Galilee. Again, we cannot but feel,
as we examine the story of the Passion, that the various
episodes had been pre-arranged. At every step the adversaries of Jesus knew exactly what they had to do. They
had agents secured to watch his movements, and to col-

lect evidence that might be used against him. They had
the proceedings at the trial ordered and rehearsed, and
must have made some appointment with the governor
so that he would be ready at break of day to sit in judgment. Everything points to a plan so carefully prepared
that it evolved itself without a hindrance from start to
finish. Once more, and this perhaps is the conclusive
evidence, the time was so short that very little can have
been improvised. We speak of the Passion week, but
from the arrival of Jesus till his death on the Cross there
was an interval of only half a week. He made his entry
on Sunday, or much more likely on Monday, for he
could not set out from Jericho till the Sabbath was over,
and the toilsome journey of fifteen miles, up a steep
mountain-side all the way and through torrid heat,
could not well be accomplished in a single day. On
Thursday he stayed in Bethany till evening when he
came into the city for the Last Supper, and on Friday
he died. Thus his stay in Jerusalem was limited to two,
or at the most three days, and time must be allowed on
each of them for the long walk from Bethany and back
again. The closing period of Jesus' life is so all-important that it occupies the major part of the Gospel record. We are left with the impression that he was in
Jerusalem a considerable time, actively working as in
his ministry in Galilee. But he cannot have been present
in the city for more than a few hours altogether. Any
teaching he did was incidental. The work before him
now was not to speak about the Kingdom of God but to

bring it into being in the manner which God would himself ordain.

The hostility to him, therefore, cannot have sprung up during his brief sojourn in Jerusalem. No time was afforded him to do anything that would involve him in serious danger. Even his act in the temple, while it might provoke the official priesthood, could not be regarded as a grave offence. He had only asserted the dignity of the holy place, protesting against a sacrilege which ought never to have been permitted. The opposition to him must have been grounded on what was known of him already. The religious leaders were acquainted with the nature of his teaching and had heard much about the ardour with which multitudes were responding to him. They were alarmed by the growing success of his mission and foresaw the consequences if it were suffered to extend much further. So it had been decided that Jesus should die. The effect of the cleansing of the temple was only to confirm this decision and to hasten the measures for putting it into action.

It was necessary first of all to collect evidence on which he could be accused, and for this purpose a number of questions were put to him, so framed as to entrap him into dangerous statements however he answered them. He saw the snares and avoided them, not by silence or evasion but by raising the issue in every case to a higher plane. He was asked, for instance, whether it was right to pay tribute to Caesar. This was the most perilous of all the questions, for if he said "no" he would at once confess himself a rebel, if he said "yes" he would alienate the mass of the people whom he relied on for support. He committed himself to neither side but only declared that the duty to God is paramount. Caesar must receive what belongs to him but men must think first of their service to God. It has been held that Jesus merely turned aside the question, which was clearly of the first importance, whatever may have been the motives that prompted it. But he gave it a straightforward answer, which affords the one possible solution to the great problem of reconciling the civil with the religious duties.

We are given to understand that all the efforts to convict him out of his own mouth were fruitless, but this cannot have been wholly so. His accusers at the trial were able to bring forward various witnesses whose evidence was conflicting but was based on words he had really uttered. Above all, there was the crucial saying: "I will destroy the temple and re-build it." We have had occasion already to consider this saying and must presently return to it, but he must have spoken it in the course of that controversy which followed the cleansing. Some question had been raised concerning the temple, with the purpose of ensnaring Jesus, and apparently it succeeded. He was led to give utterance to those highly suspicious words.

One thing seems evident, that the questions all turned on the authority of Jesus. His enemies perceived that this was the vital issue on which they must attack him. The divine requirements had been set forth plainly in the scriptures and the Law and the holy ordinances. This man was bent on changing what had always been accepted as final. Much of his teaching might seem plausible, and this was freely admitted by the more open-minded of the scribes and Pharisees; but what was the assumption that lay behind it? Jesus had claimed the right to revise the old commandments and sometimes to set them aside and put his own in place of them. What was his authority? The ultimate reason why the religious leaders were opposed to him must be sought, not in anything he expressly said or did, but in the personal claim which he had implicitly made. He had presumed, as his adversaries say of him in the Fourth Gospel, to make himself equal to God.*

The chief priests, then, collected their evidence and proceeded to action. They had first to ensure that at the right moment they might lay hands on him without the knowledge of the people, and this could be done only through someone who was personally in touch with him. It has often seemed incredible that one of Jesus' own disciples should betray him, but we have learned much in our own time of the subtle arts by which traitors can be procured in the most unlikely places, and these arts were now exercised on Judas of Kerioth, probably by venerable men whose good faith he took for granted. By his treachery, Jesus was arrested secretly by the temple police and was led for trial before the Coun-

* Jn. 5:18.

cil which was hastily assembled under the presidency of
Caiaphas the high-priest. Little is told us of this trial
in the Fourth Gospel, which lays all the stress on the
subsequent one before the Roman governor. The reason
no doubt is that in this second trial the highest earthly
power, in the person of Caesar's representative, sat in
judgment on Jesus and condemned him. The voice of
the Council was merely that of a small section of the
Jewish people and had none of that cosmic significance
which John attributes to all that concerned the death
of Jesus. But in historical fact it was the first trial which
was the decisive one. All that Pilate was called on to
do was to endorse the judgment of the Council which
was the recognised court on matters of Jewish law. He
had no knowledge of Jesus or of the grounds on which
he had been condemned. The accusation as it was presented to him was not the real one. It is in the trial
before the Council that we must seek the true explanation of why Jesus was put to death.

The fullest account of the trial is that contained in
Mark's Gospel, and there is no reason to doubt that in
the main it is trustworthy. This has been questioned
since the Council met behind closed doors, and its proceedings could not be definitely known. But its members were not sworn to secrecy and would be anxious
at a later time to justify their verdict and show that all
necessary forms had been duly observed. Moreover, a
number of witnesses had been called in and would
freely report what they had heard and seen. The record,
as we have it, bears all the intrinsic marks of truthful-

ness. An imaginary account, devised by Jesus' own followers, would have insisted on his innocence and on the flagrant injustice of those who condemned him. But the impression is given us in Mark's report that he was tried impartially. Witnesses were examined and their evidence was sifted and was set aside when it was not satisfactory. Even when it told most heavily against the prisoner a doubt was raised on a mere point of verbal disagreement. If there is prejudice in the record it might seem to be rather in favour of the judges, who apparently did their utmost in the endeavour to be strictly fair. One might almost say that what is given us is the official report of the trial, and although it is formal and incomplete, we can at least rely on it for the bare facts.

The Council, it must always be borne in mind, had a twofold function. It was a religious court, composed of the chief priests and of some eminent scribes who advised them in the interpretation of the Law. It was also a civil court, entrusted by the Romans with the maintenance of justice. There have been many instances in history of religious courts which had also a judicial power, and the combination of the two offices has always resulted in the misuse of both. Laws have been perverted in the supposed interests of religion, and religion has been subordinated to political ends. The Jewish Council was in this ambiguous position, all the more so as the Mosaic Law, on which all judgments were based, was a civil as well as a religious code. The court itself was never quite certain of the motives which gov-

erned its decisions. We have to reckon further, in the
trial of Jesus, with the obligation of the Council to
preserve the Roman peace. We are told in the Fourth
Gospel of a preliminary meeting at which some of the
members said quite frankly, "If we let this man alone
the Romans will come and take away our place and
nation." The high-priest Caiaphas was alive to this pos-
sibility. "It is expedient," he said, "that one man should
die for the people, and that the whole nation perish
not." * We cannot doubt that a consideration of this
kind was present in the minds of those who condemned
Jesus. He had started a movement which might give
rise to an insurrection, and for this the administrative
Council would be called to account. On this ground, the
Crucifixion has sometimes been regarded as a purely
political crime. The interest of the priestly rulers was
to keep themselves in power, and they sacrificed Jesus
to the security of the foreign government on which
they depended.

The political object may have had some weight with
the Council, and it was certainly put foremost when
the case was submitted to Pilate. Yet it would be unjust
to regard the chief priests as merely a group of time-
servers who curried favour with their foreign masters
by consigning their own countryman to a cruel death
on a charge of sedition. They were fully aware that
instead of gratifying the Roman magistrate they would
have difficulty in persuading him to confirm their sentence. Whatever may have been its political interest the

* Jn. 11:47-50.

Council was a religious court, and this was its primary function. It met in the precincts of the temple, and was bound by oath to maintain the holy Law. Some of its members, as we know from Josephus who himself belonged to their circle, were crafty ecclesiastics, intent on their party ends, but most of them, we cannot doubt, put religion above all else. They were narrow-minded in their devotion to it, but according to their lights, they viewed every matter on which they had to pass judgment as it affected the honour of God.

With this in mind, we must understand the trial of Jesus. The judges were prejudiced against him on many grounds, personal and political, but they were mainly concerned with the religious aspect of his work. He had professed himself to be a messenger of God, but had he not deluded the people with a false message? Instead of acting for God had he not rather opposed him and impiously set his own authority above that of God? Jesus was not the victim of a political quarrel which had nothing to do with his mission. It was recognised that he was a religious teacher, and the question at issue was his religion. The beliefs for which he stood were contrary to those which had been divinely sanctioned, and it was for this, in the last resort, that he was brought to trial and condemned.

The case against him was plainly stated in the formal indictment. He was accused of blasphemy, which by levitical law was a heinous crime, punishable by death. The word "blasphemy" is the Greek equivalent to a

Hebrew one which means literally "scorn" or "rejection." It might be applied to that contempt of one's neighbour which Jesus himself denounces in the Sermon on the Mount. "Whoever says to his brother 'Thou fool' shall be in danger of hell fire." But the word had come to have the specific meaning of an impious attitude towards God. It answers in some degree to the Greek idea of "hubris"—that arrogance by which men presume to over-step the limits set to mortals and thereby draw down on them the divine vengeance. The Hebrew idea of God was far loftier and more intense than the Greek one, and any insult to him, in language or thought or action, entailed more dreadful penalties. In a broad sense, therefore, blasphemy consisted in any encroachment on the rights of God, any attempt to seize the power or the glory which he had reserved for himself alone. This meaning is well illustrated by a verse in the book of Revelation which tells of the heads of the Beast, "bearing on them names of blasphemy." *
The reference is to the Roman emperors whose coins were stamped with the head of the reigning Caesar and above it the title "Divus" or "dominus et deus." A man here proclaimed himself to be divine. No one could pretend that Jesus had ever profaned the name of God, but his attitude could be regarded as one of blasphemy. He had dared to trespass on God's own domain. He had healed the sick by some mysterious power; he had substituted his commandments for those laid down in the sacred Law; he had pronounced forgiveness of their sins

* Rev. 13:1.

over notorious offenders. It is in this connection that
we first hear of the suspicion of blasphemy. Certain
scribes were present who murmured among themselves,
"Why doth this man thus speak? He blasphemeth, for
who can forgive sins but God only?" * A human being
had arrogated to himself the rights of God. The incident
seems to have taken place quite early in the ministry,
and when the accusation was once set on foot it grew
ever stronger. It was crystallised at last in the explicit
charge brought against Jesus at his trial. He had been
guilty of the sin of blasphemy, and the Law required
that he should die.

It has commonly been assumed that the ostensible
charge was only a pretext. The real offence of Jesus had
been that he claimed to be the Messiah. It was this that
had aroused the fierce anger of his enemies, but for
some reason they were afraid to speak of it openly and
condemned him on a vague charge which was sufficient
for their purpose, although it was not the graver one
which they had in mind. This view might seem to be
borne out by the direct question of the high-priest
after the evidence brought forward had proved unsatis-
fying: "Art thou the Messiah, the Son of the Blessed?"
Jesus, we are told, then answered plainly: "I am; and
ye shall see the Son of man sitting on the right hand of
Power." On this the high-priest exclaimed "Ye have
heard the blasphemy," and sentence was passed without
a dissenting voice.† It has been held that the incident

* Matt. 9:3.
† Mk. 14:61-64.

cannot be authentic. Jesus had evidently resolved to keep silent, and all efforts to make him speak, at this trial and the later one, were fruitless. Would he alter his decision at the crucial moment when he knew that the words he uttered would seal his doom? The high-priest's question, too, was grossly illegal. Jesus was being tried on a specific charge, and no judge had the right to discard it all of a sudden and substitute a different one. All this must be admitted, and the incident must always remain doubtful. Yet the rest of Mark's account seems to be true to historical fact, and we cannot lightly reject this part of it. The question put to Jesus was not irrelevant, for he had been accused of blasphemy and a claim to Messiahship might fairly come under this head. He had determined to say nothing, but might well feel that at this point he had no choice but to speak out. Even if he had refused to answer his silence would be construed as an admission.

It need not be assumed, however, that the Messianic claim was the real issue. If it had been so there was no reason why it should not have been definitely stated. In the trial before Pilate the whole emphasis was laid on it; why should it have been disguised at the previous trial? There was no want of sufficient evidence. Many of Jesus' actions, and very notably his cleansing of the temple, had clearly indicated that he thought of himself as the Messiah. Not only so, but the chief priests had an indubitable witness in their hands. Judas who had betrayed his Master would not have hesitated to divulge the secret confided to the disciples, and no doubt had already done so. Why was he not put forward as the star witness at the trial? We can be sure that his employers were not restrained by any fine regard for his feelings. They did not produce him because his evidence was not necessary. The question of the Messiahship was only a side-issue, for the crime of which Jesus was accused was that of blasphemy. This charge, it must be insisted, was no mere pretext concealing a much graver one. In the eyes of the judges blasphemy was by far the deadlier charge. The Messianic idea had always been a vague one. Even in the Old Testament it is construed in various ways, and later thinkers had interpreted it almost in any sense they pleased. Men had already come forward who laid claim to Messiahship and had been left at liberty. A pretender of this kind, not long after the time of Jesus, found his chief supporter in Akiba, the greatest of the Rabbis. So it was not for calling himself the Messiah, as any crazy enthusiast might have done, that Jesus was put on trial. This might aggravate his offence but by itself it did not greatly matter. His guilt consisted not in his claim to the title but in the meaning he had read into it. Professing himself the Messiah he had infringed on the rights of God. He had dared to question the laws and institutions which God had established. His claim to Messiahship might only be madness or folly, but on the strength of it he had practised blasphemy, and this was the unpardonable sin.

Thus the real point at issue in the trial of Jesus was his authority. Whatever might be the title he assumed he was seeking to over-ride the approved beliefs. He was

demanding that his word should be accepted as final in
matters that concerned the higher life. It is this that
gives a lasting significance to that trial before the Council, for it marked the beginning of a conflict which has
never ceased. Must the authority of Jesus be placed
above all others? That is ultimately the question on
which the world has been divided ever since he came.
The debate has never been fiercer than in our own time,
when so many new authorities, political, economic,
scientific, are struggling for the leadership. Can we still
believe, in face of all the hostile judgments, that Jesus
has the sovereign claim to our obedience?

Many witnesses appeared before the Council, but
there was one evidence which was manifestly the weight-
iest. Several men came forward—Matthew says two but
Mark suggests a number—who gave much the same testi-
mony: "We heard him say, I will destroy this temple
that is made with hands, and in three days I will build
another, made without hands." * The men are described
as "false witnesses," but this only implies, as the context
shows, that they wrested the words of Jesus from their
true intention and reported them somewhat differently.
Jewish law required that no evidence could be accepted
unless two or three were in full agreement, and these
witnesses were at variance as to the exact terms of Jesus'
saying. Much more was here involved than a legal
quibble about words. Had Jesus only said in a general
way "The temple may perish but another will rise in its

* Mk. 14:58.

stead?" Such a saying might be offensive to Jewish ears, but no one could take exception to it. The temple had already been restored several times over, and the same thing might happen again. But had the words been "I will destroy the temple and with little delay I will re-build it?" An utterance of this kind would plainly be blasphemous. A man would declare that he was Lord over the temple where God dwelt in very presence. He would claim the power to destroy and re-make it at his pleasure, and a claim of this kind would be an open defiance of God.

Any words can be broken from their connection and so quoted as to convey a wrong impression. This has been the favourite device of false witnesses in every age, and it was employed by those spies of the priesthood who testified against Jesus. But it cannot be doubted, as we have already seen, that Jesus spoke the words attributed to him, or something very like them. It may be gathered, too, from the outcries at the Crucifixion and at the arrest of Stephen, that Mark comes nearest to what Jesus had actually said. He had not made some abstract statement but had distinctly affirmed that he himself would destroy and rebuild the temple. He had come to make possible the true spiritual worship. Temples and ceremonies, all outward forms of religion, were only symbols. He was seeking to lead men beyond them to the reality.

The chief priests must have had some perception of the true import of the saying. If they had taken it as a literal threat to pull down the existing temple and

erect a better one they could only have concluded that
Jesus was a madman whose ravings meant nothing. But
they clearly saw that in figurative language he had attacked the established type of worship of which they
were the official guardians. His object was nothing less
than to inaugurate a new religion. This was what they
had suspected from the first, and if he had been rightly
reported he had confessed this in so many words. If it
was blasphemy to speak lightly of anything sacred, what
could be said of one who declared that the temple itself
must go? The temple stood for religion, and this man
was bent on its destruction.

We must be just to those priests who sat in judgment
on Jesus. They were not actuated merely by personal
spite or political prudence. They were not ignorant
bigots, unable with their feeble intelligence to apprehend the far-reaching purpose of Jesus. On the contrary,
they perceived it, perhaps more clearly than his own
disciples. They saw what his teaching involved in its
ultimate issues. It would lead to a new kind of religion
which would displace that which they honestly believed
to be the true one, ordained by God himself. As the
responsible heads of the faith of Israel they felt that
they must remove this menace which now hung over it.
Jesus with his new gospel had won crowds of followers,
and if he were left alone might soon pervert the whole
nation. He was putting a new authority in place of that
which had always been recognised as final. The chief
priests were conscious, as they sat in judgment, that

everything they most revered was now in peril—not only the temple and the hopes of Israel but religion itself.

The trial before the Council was the essential one. It was there that the real offence of Jesus was stated and examined, and the decision arrived at that he must be put to death. But the judicial power of the Council had this limitation, that a capital sentence could not be carried into effect without the sanction of the Roman governor. This served to remind the subject people that while they were allowed their own legal system, the final authority was in the hands of Rome. Jesus was therefore brought before Pilate, not so much for a second trial as for the endorsement of the sentence passed on him. This, however, placed the Council in a grave difficulty. It had condemned Jesus on a charge of blasphemy, which under Jewish law was a capital crime, but for a Roman judge would be meaningless. The case had therefore to be presented to him in a form he could understand, and all emphasis was now thrown on Jesus' claim to be Messiah. He had set himself up as a national king, a rival to Caesar. This, it has often been pointed out, was a plain distortion of the charge on which he had been condemned, but the accusers could fairly argue that they were only stating it in different terms. Jesus had been convicted of blasphemy, of usurping the rights of God; and in so doing he had defied all authority, earthly as well as divine. If his pretensions were admitted there would be an end to all the governments which held society together. It was this aspect of his offence which was now impressed on the Roman magistrate. The charge of blasphemy was not abandoned but was thrown into language which would be intelligible even to a Pagan. This prisoner had been condemned because he aspired to a sovereignty which would nullify that of Caesar.

Confirmation of a sentence was usually granted with little question. It could be assumed that a Jewish court was the best qualified to pass judgment in Jewish affairs, and a sensible governor accepted its decisions. But Jesus was accused of sedition, and this, for the ruling power, was a matter of serious consequence. It has sometimes been held that the Gospel writers have magnified the part of Pilate in the great tragedy. He is represented as deeply concerned and as hesitating long before he pronounced his sentence. Is it not more probable that amidst the business which crowded on him during his brief annual visit to Jerusalem he hardly gave a thought to this obscure quarrel of Jewish religious parties? A famous French author * has imagined him as proudly reviewing his term of office a few years afterwards. His friend asks him whether there was not a singular incident connected with one Jesus; to which he can only answer, "I do not remember it." But it is impossible that he can have treated the case of Jesus as merely one of ordinary routine. The prisoner was accused as a leader of insurrection, and the paramount duty of a Roman governor in that unsettled country was to pre-

* Anatole France in *Le Procurateur de Judée*.

serve the imperial rights. The faintest rumour of an outbreak had to be examined with scrupulous care. Pilate would recognise at once that he was dealing with a matter which affected the security of his province, and perhaps of the whole empire. Even if the charges against Jesus were unfounded he could not run the risk of neglecting them, for who could tell what might lie behind them. The Gospel records can be fully trusted when they represent Pilate as trying, with his utmost effort, to ascertain the facts. The Jewish leaders may have expected that he would confirm their judgment in the usual manner after a few formal questions, but the enquiry was prolonged and searching. It convinced the governor that there was no real evidence on the one matter that caused him anxiety. Whatever he may have done Jesus had not conspired against the rule of Caesar. His accusers had some grievance of a personal or purely religious nature, which lay quite outside the jurisdiction of Roman law. So instead of endorsing the sentence of the Council, Pilate wished to reverse it, in such a way, however, as not to hurt the pride of the Jewish authorities whom he had to work with and could not afford to alienate. His efforts to make a compromise broke down, and a cry arose that he was condoning an offence against the emperor. At this point he was panic-stricken and gave way. No doubt he reasoned with himself that although Jesus was only a religious fanatic yet in Palestine a religious movement was always liable to become a political one. This man had clearly obtained a dangerous influence over the people and he might use it eventually for doubtful ends. The safest course was to fall in with the judgment of the Council and have him put to death.

The men who were responsible for the Crucifixion have now been branded as the most hateful of all criminals. Their names have become symbols of injustice, treachery, cruelty, utter perversion of the moral law. Dante has summed up the world's judgment when he places them in the lowest depths of hell. But it is well to remind ourselves that they were all conscientious men, acting, they believed, for the best. The Pharisees were faithful to the Law in which God had expressed his holy will, and they could not but oppose Jesus, who had called the Law in question. The chief priests were the guardians of the temple and felt it to be their sacred duty to punish the man who was bent on destroying it. Pilate represented the emperor and was bound to protect his interests in a rebellious land. Judas had no doubt been persuaded that he would do a service to his country by handing over to the rightful authorities one who was bringing it into peril. Perhaps it is the chief tragedy of the Crucifixion that it was not the work of criminals but of men who were earnestly trying, according to their lights, to do what was right. This has always been one of the tragedies of human life. More often than not the worst evils have been wrought by well-meaning men. This is brought home to us as we study the history of the past, and we see examples of it daily in the lives of men around us. All of us, when we have performed the actions with which we feel most satisfied, have need of the prayer, "Father, forgive them, for they know not what they do."

It is very remarkable that Paul, although his one theme is the death of Christ, makes no allusion to the human agents through whom it was effected. The only apparent reference is in his account of the Lord's Supper: "Our Lord Jesus, on that night on which he was betrayed," and the Greek word he uses has only the general sense, "he was given over." * Elsewhere Paul speaks of God as giving up his Son for our salvation, and this, most probably, is his thought here. He reminds us that the Supper was ordained on the very night when God made the great surrender of his Son. For Paul, those who were really responsible for the death of Christ were "the rulers of this world," † the invisible powers which are behind all evil and employ men as their unconscious instruments. This is indeed the ultimate explanation of why Christ died. His death was brought about by no historical accident but was the final outcome of those forces of evil which are inherent in the very constitution of things and over-rule our actions even when they aim at what is good. Nevertheless, the condemnation of Jesus was an event in history, and has to be related to historical men and circumstances. Not only so, but it resulted, as an event in history always does, from a whole series of events which led up to it. The French Revolution, the civil wars in England and America, the two great wars of our own time, appeared to break out

* 1 Cor. 11:23.
† 1 Cor. 2:8.

suddenly, and we can fix on a definite incident in each case which brought about the catastrophe. But this incident in itself was of minor importance. It only gave the final impulse to a conflict which had long been preparing. The dangerous material had all been accumulated and only needed the spark to set it in flames.

The cleansing of the temple may be regarded as the incident which brought the hostility to Jesus to a head, and we can hardly doubt that he so intended it. He deliberately threw down his challenge to those whom he recognised as his real enemies. They had long been working against him in the background, and he now insisted that they should meet him openly. They had no choice but to accept his defiance, and their policy of intrigue had now to be laid aside. When once they were driven to action they proceeded with headlong speed, and within three days after his cleansing of the temple he was arrested and tried and executed. But this haste was possible because there had been long preparation. We cannot understand the events which followed the cleansing unless we relate them to that opposition which Jesus had encountered ever since he began his work.

We must not say, therefore, that the death of Jesus was directly due to his action in the temple. It sometimes happens that the struggle for a great cause is let loose by a mere accident, some outbreak of passion which has little to do with the question at issue but which takes place at a critical moment when even a small thing may open the flood-gates. The act of Jesus has sometimes been regarded in this light. It has been held that when he cleansed the temple he lost sight for the time being of his true mission. The temple ritual was no concern of his, but he was hurried by an impulse of indignation into an action which was unnecessary and which brought down on him the wrath of the priest-hood and so occasioned his death. Thus he died, not in the fulfilment of his purpose, but in consequence of his rash interference in matters which lay outside of his province. But he acted, as we have seen, after a night's reflection, with a full knowledge of what he was doing and of what the effects might be. His action in the temple cannot be regarded as a mere minor episode which happened at such a time and in such circumstances that it gave rise to momentous events. Jesus intended by means of it to bring his mission to a head. Of his own accord he set in motion that chain of consequences which were to have their issue in his death.

For this reason alone it is highly significant, and places the whole Gospel history in a new light. In the great struggle that now lay before him Jesus took the initiative. He knew that his enemies were preparing to attack him and he struck first and compelled them to meet him on ground of his own choosing. He is represented in the Fourth Gospel as himself determin-ing all that should befall him, so that those who cap-tured and slew him were only carrying out his will while he seemed to be helpless in their hands. This is a theo-logical view and is apt to impress us as utterly false and artificial. Yet at the heart of it there is an historical truth. Jesus was not the passive victim of forces too strong for him. He did not go blindly as a sheep to the slaughter. In a real sense he acted by his own will and was the master of those powers which appeared to have him at their mercy. This he made evident by his cleansing of the temple. He thereby decided how his enemies would have to proceed against him. He defined the issue on which they would have to meet them and forced them to accept it. All that happened afterwards, we may truly say, had been willed by Jesus himself.

His act was significant, however, not only because of its consequences but in its own intrinsic meaning. We can be sure that when Jesus resolved to do something that would bring his cause to a final decision he would not content himself with a petty act which had no importance in itself, although it might provide a starting-point for great events. He would seek to perform an action which in some way would illuminate his purpose and put the seal on all that he had hitherto said and done, so that the conflict now impending should be fought out on the central issues. We have thus to consider the larger significance of that cleansing of the temple.

Chapter Eight

HISTORICAL AND RELIGIOUS VALUE

It has been the misfortune of our religion from the very beginning, that the different elements in the work of Jesus have been separated. This, indeed, is a tribute to his greatness. He achieved so much, his interests were so many-sided, that he cannot be comprehended in his totality. In every attempt to explain him some one aspect of his mission has been taken by itself and we have had countless presentations of Jesus, with little resemblance to each other and yet all of them, in their measure, authentic. But the danger has always been that some one part of the reality should be taken for the whole. Paul asked the Corinthians, when he saw them breaking into sects under the banners of their several teachers, "Is Christ divided?" * Surely he was one, and his work, if it was rightly understood, must be all of a piece, each aspect of it harmonious with all the others. Yet men have always been dividing him. They have seen in him two separate natures, divine and human. They

* 1 Cor. 1:13.

have drawn a line between his ethical and his purely religious teaching. They have distinguished between a permanent meaning in his message and one that was valid only for a given age. He has been so divided that it becomes ever more difficult to form any conception of what he really was.

The story of his life has been confused, like his message, by this inability to grasp it as a whole. It is assumed that the earlier part of his ministry was quite distinct from the later one. After he had worked for a time in Galilee as a wandering teacher his activity suddenly took a different turn, and he went up to Jerusalem in the character of the Messiah, divinely appointed to bring in the Kingdom. There seems to be no relation between these two parts of his career. Apparently he gave up his original purpose and devoted himself to a new one, and this, it has sometimes been held, was his grand mistake. Instead of continuing the quiet work which was growing ever more fruitful, he started on a wild enterprise which could only result in failure and death. But however it may be regarded, the later phase of his ministry seems to have no connection with the previous one. His life falls abruptly into two sections which must be kept apart.

It is evident, however, as we study the Gospel narrative, that Jesus never changed. Wherever we meet him— teaching on the mountain, healing the sick, at supper with his disciples, suffering on the Cross—we feel ourselves in contact with the same Personality, intent on the same ends. His deeds have all to be taken together and each of them helps us to understand the others. This was apparent to our evangelists, and it supplied the motive which led them to compile their record. The original Gospel, as may be gathered from many indications, consisted only of an account of the Passion. Paul seems to have confined himself to this, and in all his Epistles he never mentions Galilee or alludes to anything that had happened there. It was enough for him, as he tells the Galatians, "to set before your eyes as in a picture, Jesus Christ, crucified among you." * But the need of prefixing some account of the life to this recital of the death soon made itself felt. It was not merely that the listeners were curious to know more of this divine Person who had died for them, but they realised that this knowledge was necessary if the story of the death was to be intelligible. There must have been something in the life which brought about the death and threw light on its meaning and purpose. The aim of the evangelists is to provide this background to the Passion story. They perceive that the earlier and the later events are knit together. From the first they have their eyes fixed on the death of Jesus, but in their record of how he had lived they prepare us for understanding why he died.

The history of Jesus, therefore, does not fall into two sections which have to be kept separate from one another. All that happened in the later period is integrally connected with what had gone before. This is brought

* Gal. 3:1.

home to us by the cleansing of the temple. More than anything else in the Gospels it seems to stand out as an incident by itself and for this reason has been called in question. It is argued that Jesus would not have performed an act which had no bearing on his mission, which was out of keeping with his known character, which was certain to excite hostility when he was most in need of friends. Doubts of this kind might be raised about particular actions of many famous men, for instance that of Cromwell when he purged the House of Commons, which to his mind had grown corrupt. He said of the mace "Take away that bauble," much as Jesus had said "Take these things hence." It might well be held that an act so arbitrary and in many ways so injudicious cannot be credited and must have been foisted by popular legend on the memory of a great man. But no one can question it, and it is not difficult to explain when we take account of the long struggle which it finally brought to a head. In a similar manner we must regard the act of Jesus. It does not stand by itself but must be brought into relation with previous events which had made it necessary.

So far, therefore, from being a mere interruption it may be taken as the essential link between the two parts of Jesus' ministry, at first sight entirely separate from each other. He had been engaged on a work which he was now to carry to its fulfilment, and performed an act which was the outcome of what he had already done and prepared the way for what he was still to do. We have seen that while he taught in Galilee he was all the time feeling his way to the conviction that he was not merely the prophet of the Kingdom but the Messiah who was destined to bring it in. He had divulged his secret to the inner circle of his disciples and now took the decisive step of acting in the character of the Messiah. His course from this moment was marked out for him. We have seen, too, that by his act in the temple he exposed his enemies and compelled them to come forward. So the incident not only relates itself to the previous history but supplies a key to much in it that is perplexing. Almost from the outset Jesus had been faced with an opposition which grew ever more dangerous; what were the forces behind it? This is never explained, but we know for a fact that it was the chief priests who finally compassed his death. There is at least a presumption that they had been his real enemies all along, working against him by various hidden means. This can hardly be questioned when we find him beginning his mission at Jerusalem by an open challenge to them. He declared by this emphatic action that it was they who had ever been opposing him and that they must now come forward without disguise and decide the issue.

The incident thus explains the conditions under which he had been working, and it also throws a vivid light on his own character. Far too often the whole stress has been laid on his patience and gentleness. With his finer nature he was helpless amidst the wrongs and cruelties of this rough world and could only submit to them without a murmur. There is much in the record

that might seem to bear out this conception of him. He
describes himself as meek and lowly of heart; he exhorts
his followers to turn the other cheek to the smiter; he
condemns all pride and self-assertion; he gives perfect
fulfilment to the prophet's vision of the Suffering Servant.* Everywhere in the New Testament he is held up
as the grand example of patient endurance; "when he
was reviled he reviled not again, when he suffered he
threatened not." † The picture is touching and beauti-
ful, but it has often been felt that with all his goodness
he was somewhat wanting in the more virile qualities.
Our love and admiration are mingled with a certain
pity and it is this emotion, more than any other,
which many great painters have sought to evoke in their
portrayal of his face.

The chief reason why the incident of the cleansing
has often been viewed suspiciously is that it is so contrary to the conventional idea of Jesus. He appears on
this one occasion as acting with a strong hand. According to John's account he drove out the traffickers with
a scourge, and even when this detail is ruled out his
action was one of violence. He did not persuade or
remonstrate but boldly enforced his will. Such a method,
we are told, was utterly out of keeping with the character of Jesus. But when we form an estimate of any
man, all his known actions must be taken into account,
and it stands on record that Jesus performed this one.
We have no right to leave it out of consideration be-

* Matt. 12:17 f.
† 1 Pet. 2:23.

cause it seems to contradict the others. We have rather
to admit that our previous judgment has been defective
and must be revised so as to make room for this action
also. It is significant for many reasons, and not least for
this—that it discloses one side of Jesus' nature which
might be overlooked when we contemplate the rest of
the history. Behind his gentleness and forbearance there
was a reserve of strength and fiery resolution. Something
is added here which gives a new meaning to all that is
told us of his patience under suffering. We can see that
it was rooted, not in a sense of helplessness under evils
which it was vain to withstand, but in a consciousness
of power. With all his strength he was able to restrain
himself. When this is understood, we perceive the real
meaning of many of those acts and sayings which might
seem to indicate a strain of softness in his nature. When
he calls himself meek and lowly he only declares that
he is not arrogant but is willing to lend his support even
to the humblest. When he bids us not to resist evil he
is speaking, as the context shows, of mere personal in-
juries. All that matters is the great cause of God in
which we are enlisted, and like brave soldiers we are
not to mind the buffets and discomforts which may
befall ourselves. He describes himself in the Fourth
Gospel as the Good Shepherd, and the ordinary conception of his tenderness is largely based on this parable.
But the word "good" is used in the sense in which we
still apply it to a good workman or seaman or physician.
He claims for himself that he is no pretender. He is a
real shepherd, not a hireling, and the whole aim of the

parable is to impress on us that a good shepherd thinks only of his duty and will defend his flock against wolves and robbers although it costs him his life. The idea of tenderness does not enter into the thought at all.

If there is one quality which may be singled out as the distinctive one in the character of Jesus it is not his gentleness but his indomitable courage. If this had not been so, he would never have died on the Cross. He knew in the closing days that it was in store for him but he made no effort to escape; and when he was offered the opiate which would have dulled his torment he would not take it. He had the same kind of courage as those brave men who have refused to be blindfolded when they faced the firing-squad. That is how we find him all through his history when we once free ourselves of the idea that he was a frail victim, unequal to the burden laid upon him. He never allowed himself to be overcome. He met every trial with a calm courage, and it was courage above all else that he demanded from his followers. Again and again he warned them that their task would be a hard one. They would be mocked and scourged and rejected and dragged before judges and kings. In face of these perils they were not to tremble or give way. It was not meekness that he required of them but an unflinching courage, and he offered himself as their example.

The action in the temple, therefore, was not out of keeping with the character of Jesus. On the contrary, it was all of a piece with that quality in him which can be traced clearly in all that he said and did. He drove out the traders and money-changers just as he had spoken fearlessly against scribes and Pharisees, against the rich and powerful, against all hypocrisies and evil customs and vain traditions. He was indeed gentle and forgiving but never hesitated on a right occasion to utter words of wrath and indignation, and he who could speak in that manner was also prepared to act. It is sometimes assumed that he was radically opposed to all kinds of violence, and this, for many people, is one of the primary Christian principles. Whatever you do to your fellow-man you must not treat him roughly, and war is wrong because it employs the method of physical force. But what Jesus condemned was the spirit of hatred in whatever way it might manifest itself. It may have its outcome in quarrel and blood-shed or merely in slanders and crafty scheming, but the hatred which prompts the deed is the essential sin. So, in the view of Jesus, violence was not in itself an evil. He allowed for times, as we can gather from some of his parables, when a right purpose is futile unless it gives rise to a violent act. It is indeed incredible that he took a scourge to expel the money-changers, but the objection to this detail in John's narrative is not that Jesus was opposed on principle to all forms of violence. We may be sure that he would not have scrupled to use a whip if he could not have put down a glaring sacrilege in any other way. Indeed the very fact that this addition found a place in the story is highly significant. At a time when the memory of Jesus was still fresh the idea that he acted violently was not felt to be incongruous. Those who

had known him were aware that this was how he might
have acted. He had left the impression of a strong-
armed, determined man, who would not have held back,
when force was necessary, from strenuous action.

So the incident in the temple, so far from conflicting
with the previous record, is in full accord with it, and
brings out one aspect of it which is too often left out
of sight. Jesus was not the ineffectual visionary whom
modern sentimentalists have imagined. The knights of
the Middle Ages were far nearer the truth when they
saw in him the pattern of chivalry, the strong man who
was also gentle, employing his strength for the defence
of the weak and the assertion of right against all tyranny
and injustice. This conception of him must ever be
borne in mind as we read the Gospels. The tender, long-
suffering Jesus whom they set before us was also he
who defied the chief priests in their citadel and put fear
into a crowd of evil-doers. He had both these sides to
his nature, and they have both to be taken together.

The incident gives us insight into his character, and
also into the work to which he set himself. Here too it
provides a key to the previous record. At first sight it
seems to have little connection with it and even to contradict it; but when we look deeper, it confirms the
story of the ministry and throws new light on its nature
and purpose.

In the first place, Jesus began his mission in Jerusalem by a conspicuous action. Hitherto he had worked
quietly as a teacher, seeking by word and example to

change the minds of men and prepare them for the
Kingdom of God. Now he came forward in a new character and enforced his will by an emphatic act. This,
for many, has been the chief difficulty in the incident.
It seems inconsistent with all we have previously heard
of the work of Jesus. Men had observed that he was
averse to all outward displays of power. He was convinced that little could be achieved by forcible action,
and that men required to be inwardly changed. It was
to this work of renewing the mind and heart that he
devoted all his effort. But it is just at this point that the
incident serves to correct a grave error in our conception of his ministry. We are apt to think of him, especially in our day, as primarily a teacher, who gave us
new ideas of priceless value as to the nature of God, and
of human personality, and of the right conduct of life.
He is classed with other great thinkers, and it is shown
where he agreed with them and where he differed. Some
writers have contended that he went fatally wrong when
he gave up his work of teaching and offered himself as
a Messianic leader. They would have us forget this
aberration and fix our minds wholly on the glorious
things he taught. But if we take an attitude of this kind
we miss the whole intention of Jesus. He has to be
classified, if this is thought necessary, not with the great
thinkers but with the men of action. It was not ideas
that he gave us but deeds of his own, in the strength of
which we can do others like them. Everywhere in his
teaching he lays all the stress on action, and he regards
his words as only the means to action. Among those

who listened to him there were many who admired his ideas and declared that no other man spoke like him, but for tributes of this kind he cared nothing. "He who heareth my words and doeth them not is like a man who built his house upon the sand." * The ideas were nothing unless they took the form of acts. He presented his message most often by means of things he did, only adding his words in order to point their significance. It is often objected to the Gospels that they give so much attention to the miracles, which to our minds, however we regard them, are only incidental to the real message. We would gladly exchange most of those miracle stories for a few more of the immortal sayings which take us into the mind of Jesus and disclose how he thought of God and of the mysteries of life and death. But in recounting the miracles the evangelists are guided by a true instinct. They realise that the ministry of Jesus was essentially one of action. His teaching all depends on things he did, and must be so regarded before we can understand it. He had come not merely to instruct but actually to do something which would make the world different.

It has always been remarked as very strange that so little is said in the later New Testament books about the teaching of Jesus. All the counsels offered in these books are based on that teaching, and in several places Paul refers directly to sayings of the Lord, showing that he had knowledge of them. Yet the emphasis in Paul's writings and in all the others is on the redeeming work

* Matt. 7:26.

which Christ had done, and what he taught seems almost
to be forgotten. From this, it has been inferred that the
whole character of Jesus' religion had somehow changed.
He had appeared as a teacher but had been transformed
into the maker of a new life, and so to think of him
had become the essence of Christian faith. But the New
Testament writers have truly understood the purpose
of Jesus. His mind was set on effecting a great work to
which God had appointed him. His teaching was only
a part of his work, just as laying a foundation is part
of the erection of a great building. The church in the
later time looked only at the building as it now stood
complete.

The cleansing of the temple was in many ways a striking act, but perhaps its chief significance lay just in
this—that it was an act. Jesus now declared in a way
there could be no mistaking that he was no visionary,
intent on ideals which could not be realised in a practical world. He had come to make a visible change in
present conditions, and all this time, while men thought
of him only as a teacher, he had been working towards
that end. His purpose had been one of action, and now
he made this clear by a manifest act. His enemies could
not but see his intention. They had long felt that he was
dangerous but while he confined himself to words they
could persuade themselves that he would do little harm.
Gamaliel, shortly afterwards, advised the Council not
to interfere with the Apostles since false opinions would
soon die down of their own accord.* Many were no

* Ac. 5:38.

doubt inclined to take a similar attitude to Jesus himself. Now, however, he had proceeded to action, and his previous teaching at once stood out in a different light. It had to be taken seriously. His aim was quite evidently to break down the existing order, and to put something different in its place. It was the positive act of Jesus which revealed the true nature of his work, and this was why he performed it. He wished to make it clear that he was no dreamer and had meant everything that he had said. He was bent on effecting those mighty changes which he had foretold.

He wished also that his act should indicate, in a sort of parable, the nature of those changes for which he was working. There might seem to be little relation between the message of Jesus, as it appears in the Sermon on the Mount, and his cleansing of the temple. We are struck, rather, with the obvious contrast. He had declared that nothing matters but purity of heart, mercy and forgiveness, inner obedience to the will of God. In this way alone can men become the children of their Father who is in heaven. Yet he apparently came forward as the champion of ritual purity. He saw in the temple the very house of God and would not endure the least infringement on its holy ordinances. Must we not conclude that while he rose above many of the narrow conceptions of his time he never really broke away from the old traditions? It was only in a later retrospect that he came to be viewed as the bringer of a message which was essentially new. All that he aimed at was to restore Judaism to what he conceived to be its true character, and this he signified by cleansing the temple.

Now it may be granted that much can be said for this interpretation of Jesus. He said explicitly that he came not to destroy the Law but to fulfil it. He owed much to the Rabbis and the apocalyptic thinkers, not to speak of the Old Testament itself. Some parallel to almost all his sayings is to be found in the earlier Jewish literature. His followers in all times have been far too eager to make out that he said nothing that was not wholly original, as if his thoughts must lose their value if they had entered into anyone's mind before him. The very contrary is true. Men have always been seeking after God, and have realised, however imperfectly, what he requires of them. We know the truth when we see it because it answers to beliefs which are inborn in us and which men have held since the beginning. Jesus took his stand on them, and embodied in his own teaching the ideas and sometimes the very words of other holy men. This has always been the strength of his religion. "Everything," said Justin Martyr in the second century, "that has been wisely and truly said at any time belongs by right to us Christians." * Jesus indeed brought a new message from God but never discarded those which he had sent already. This was not his deficiency but his greatness. He clung to what was old because his mind was set on the everlasting.

He looked, however, to what was central in that old

* *2nd Apology.*

religion to which he never ceased to be faithful. His idea of fulfilling the Law was to pierce down through the letter to the inner intention, and this was the difference between him and the Pharisees. They sought to fulfil the Law by meticulous observance of all its details, while he was concerned only with its vital principles. He held that by doing good on the Sabbath, you obeyed the Sabbath law; by helping your fellow-men whenever they were in need, you satisfied all the intricate code of social obligation; by sustaining your body for God's service, you made all meats clean. He never broke with the Jewish religion but what he took over from it was religion itself, insofar as he found it under the Jewish forms. For the sake of the truth contained in it he honoured the old religion in spite of priests and Pharisees who had turned it into a vain routine.

He honoured the Law, and still more the temple. It was only an earthly house but all holy aspirations had centred on it for a thousand years. It was meant to keep the people mindful that God was in the midst of them. He was not a dread Power somewhere in the distance whom they could only know through his commandments, but he was close beside them, and they could trust in his protection. This was what the temple had meant to the Psalmists, and it had the same significance for Jesus. His reverence for it has been urged as the crowning proof that he never freed himself from old superstitions, but the belief that God is a reality, present on this earth and accessible to men in their weakness and misery, was no superstition. For Jesus it was the one truth that mattered, and he was ever seeking to make men believe it and live by it. This is recognised by the author of the Fourth Gospel, who reports few of those sayings which bear directly on moral and social duties. According to this evangelist, Jesus spoke only of the need of fellowship with God, and it has seemed to many that the real teaching, as we know it from the other Gospels, is left entirely out of sight. But what John has tried to give us is the inner substance of Jesus' message. He sees that the definite precepts were only so many illustrations or practical applications. The one concern of Jesus was that men should feel the reality of God and live always as in his presence. So in the temple he saw the visible symbol of his own primary conviction. It was only a symbol and he looked for a time when it would disappear and give place to the thing itself. He thought of his own work as hastening that time when no material house would be necessary. But meanwhile the temple stood before men's eyes as the witness that God was present with them, and it must be kept holy.

Much more, therefore, was involved in his action than that a decent reverence should be shown to things and places that are accounted sacred. If men are truly to wait on God and seek his help and guidance they must preserve their sense of his holiness. Their thought of him must not be contaminated by anything that speaks only of this world. A compass is worse than useless if it is exposed to influences that deflect it from pointing straight to the pole, and the thought of God is our compass. He alone can direct us amidst all the confusions of our earthly life. We must test our actions by his standards. We can appeal to his judgment when we are bewildered by all the conflicting counsels. His name, therefore, must be hallowed. We must keep our devotion to him separate from all our lower passions and interests. It has been the fundamental error of religion in all times to combine the worship of God with national pride and ambition, with the desire for personal advantage and worldly success. "Ye cannot," said Jesus, "serve God and Mammon" and he put his word into action when he cleansed the temple. Those traffickers were engaged in their ordinary business, and in this there was nothing wrong. They sold their wares for a religious use and might fairly claim that while making a profit for themselves they were also assisting in the worship of God. But no true service of him is possible without the sense that he is the Holy One, judging this world because he is high above its wrangling and turmoil. The temple existed for the very purpose of lifting men out of their common lives and bringing them into the presence of this holy God. His worship and the pursuit of earthly things cannot be joined together.

The act of Jesus has the more significance when we remember that it was performed in the court of the Gentiles, and that he appealed to that verse of Isaiah, "My house shall be called a house of prayer for all nations." The three closing words, so strangely omitted by Matthew and Luke, contain the whole point of the prophetic saying. A day is foretold when all the peoples on earth will be one with Israel in the worship of the true God. This was also the thought of Jesus. The temple, for him, was not merely the shrine of Jewish religion, so that the outer enclosure assigned to the Gentiles might be treated as of no account. It stood for religion itself—for that assurance of God which all men were seeking for. So Jesus did not act in the interest of a particular religious system to which he was still devoted in spite of his broader outlook. He was asserting a principle on which all true religion must be founded. There can be no communion with God unless the worship of him is kept unpolluted.

Perhaps the best commentary on Jesus' action, in its deeper implications, is that which is given us in the Epistle to the Hebrews. The writer of this remarkable book sets himself to discover what had been the ultimate meaning of the work of Christ, and he takes his guidance from the ordinances of the tabernacle, which later had become the temple. He sees the purpose of Christ typified in those ordinances, divinely appointed. The sanctuary on earth was the counterpart in material form of a heavenly one into which Christ has ascended to minister as our great High-Priest. He has given reality to all that was fore-shadowed in the ancient symbolism. The argument of the Epistle is often fanciful and artificial, and is helped out by Greek-philosophical ideas, but beneath it we can discern a profound insight. Jesus brought a new message, but it was that towards which all previous religion had been striving. Men were conscious of a God above them. They desired to approach

him and hold fellowship with him, and through Christ
they had at last obtained this access to God. The writer
sees in the temple the outstanding example of this age-
long endeavour to draw near to God, and he thus
connects its worship with the work of Christ. But he
might well have developed his thought, not by means
of allegory, but on the basis of historical fact. Jesus had
himself seen in the temple the visible expression of
man's longing to draw near to God. He was conscious
that this earthly sanctuary was the image of a higher
one in which men would worship the Father in spirit
and in truth. He had purified the temple in order that
its reflection of that other should not be stained and
obscured. So between the act of Jesus and the idea elab-
orated in the Epistle to the Hebrews there is a real correspondence. For the later writer the earthly sanctuary
was a type of that heavenly one in which Christ now
ministers, securing for men that access to God which
they have ever been seeking. Jesus also saw a divine
significance in the temple. It spoke to him of access to
God in a house not made with hands, and this was the
theme of his own message. For the sake of what it
pointed to, he cleansed the earthly house from a pollu-
tion.

The analogy with Hebrews can be pressed further.
As the writer of the Epistle compares the earthly and
the heavenly sanctuaries, so he thinks of Christ as the
true High-Priest, who holds his office by no mere accident of descent but in right of his intrinsic nature. This
was the implication in Jesus' cleansing of the temple.

He entered the holy place and took on himself the ordering of it. He was conscious within him of an authority which transcended that of the official priesthood whose rule had hitherto been undisputed. It was only the expected Messiah who could thus assert himself as Lord of the temple, and Jesus meant by his action to lay claim to that sovereign title. But his claim was grounded in his sense of a unique power inherent in his own Person. He assumed the traditional title, although in many ways it conflicted with what he knew to be his calling, for it was the only one which could express his conviction that he had the true knowledge of God, that God was acting and speaking through him, that his will must be accepted as that of God.

It was by his action in the temple that he declared his authority and thereby set in motion that sequence of events which led up to his death. We may therefore look to this incident for some clue to the great problem of why he was crucified. He had committed no crime and plotted no insurrection. Pilate, after examining the evidence, admitted freely that on these grounds there was nothing against him. He had indeed been critical of the Law but had never ceased to observe it, and there were not a few of the more liberal scribes and Pharisees who admired his teaching. Yet he had aroused such a fierce hostility that the high court of his nation decided without a dissenting voice that he must die. Why was it that he was condemned? There were no doubt many reasons, and all of them must be taken into account. He was dangerous politically in a country where any popular excitement might start a revolt. Although he had never attacked the Law, his teaching was of such a nature as to destroy its very basis. He was personally obnoxious to many of the leading men. A professional class is always jealous of interlopers, and Jesus had gained an influence with the people which was hotly resented by the men in power. Pilate perceived "that for envy they had delivered him up." * These factors must all be allowed their due weight, but none of them can have been decisive. Neither can Jesus have been crucified merely because he had professed to be the Messiah. That title could be interpreted in so many ways that by itself it signified little and others who had assumed it had been unmolested. The point at issue was not the title but the meaning which Jesus had attached to it. He had aspired to an authority which must over-rule all others. He had dared to put himself on an equality with God, and for this blasphemy he must be put to death.

It is here that we must discover the ultimate reason why Jesus was condemned. He did not die by a tragic accident as the victim of private animosities or of the peculiar conditions, religious and political, which happened at that time to exist in Palestine. A question of tremendous import was at stake, and of this his enemies were at least dimly conscious. They rightly felt that there must be some authority which men could accept

* Mk. 15:10.

as final, and they found it in the traditional system of which they were the guardians. Jesus had maintained that there was a higher one. He had declared that all other powers, however self-confident, must give way to that will of God which he had revealed in his message. Which was the true authority, that which was generally accepted or this new one personified in Jesus? It was this question which was at issue in his trial, and the conflict which then began is still in process. As we read of how he was condemned to death, we feel that such an error was only possible in an ignorant and misguided age. We think sometimes how differently we should respond to him if he appeared among us now. But can we doubt that if he came again to-morrow, acting and speaking much as he did then, the old story would repeat itself with only the circumstances a little changed? There would be new priests and Pharisees and judges who would deal with him as the old ones did. They would resent his challenge to the settled authorities. They would insist on his removal in the interests of the state, and of progress, and of the social order. He was himself aware that there would always be this opposition. "When the Son of man cometh," he asked sorrowfully, "will he find faith on earth?" *

The cleansing of the temple was thus of crucial significance both for the history and the religion of Jesus. It gave the impulse to that train of events which led to his death and serves in great measure to explain them.

* Lk. 18:3.

It connects itself also with the events that had gone before and helps us to understand them. We cannot but feel as we study the Gospel record that there is a great deal which lies below the surface. Again and again Jesus makes some movement for which there is no apparent reason. We see him contending with hostile forces the nature of which is never clearly indicated. The course of the ministry is perplexing, not only because it is only described in separate episodes but because so little is told us of its background. If we were afforded some light on the conditions under which Jesus was working, of the designs of his enemies and their conspiracy against him, much that now baffles us in the history would be explained. This unwritten part of the Gospels is illuminated, at least in some of its aspects, by the incident in the temple. But it is also of the highest significance from the religious point of view. Jesus performed a Messianic act and thus declared openly what he conceived himself to be. He suggested, at the same time, in what sense he claimed to be the Messiah. He also disclosed the motives which underlay all his teaching. While he had taught in words, he had been intent on action just as now when he suppressed an evil with a strong hand. His aim had been to make God real to men, so that they might live as in his holy presence. Above all, by his cleansing of the temple he asserted his authority. He was conscious of something in himself which gave him the right to command. His authority was no arbitrary one like that of an autocrat who insists that his word must be law. He knew that he spoke for God and that what he said was in accordance with God's will. With all that was divine in their own being men could not but respond to him and obey him. This has ever been the secret of his authority. From time to time men have questioned him and turned to other leaders, but in the end they must always come back to Jesus. He speaks for God himself. He has the words of eternal life.

INDEX